Volume **17** **THE**
GOLDEN BOOK
ENCYCLOPEDIA

soap to Syria

An exciting, up-to-date encyclopedia in 20 fact-filled, entertaining volumes

Especially designed as a first encyclopedia for today's grade-school children

More than 2,500 full-color photographs and illustrations

From the Publishers of Golden® Books

Western Publishing Company, Inc.
Racine, Wisconsin 53404

ILLUSTRATION CREDITS
(t=top, b=bottom, c=center, l=left, r=right)

1 l, Fiona Reid/Melissa Turk & The Artist Network; 1 r, Smithsonian Institution; 3 b, Focus on Sports; 4, David Lindroth Inc.; 5, Brian Seed/Click/Chicago; 6 bl, Brad Hamann; 6 br, Bettmann Archive; 7 t, William Strode/Woodfin Camp; 7 inset, Lloyd P. Birmingham; 8, Tanya Rebelo/Joseph, Mindlin & Mulvey Inc.; 9 t, Andrew Rackoczy/Bruce Coleman Inc.; 9 br, NASA; 10–11 and 12, Tom Powers/Joseph, Mindlin & Mulvey Inc.; 13, NASA; 14, Michael O'Reilly/Joseph, Mindlin & Mulvey Inc.; 15 tl, Paolo Koch/Photo Researchers; 15 inset, Lloyd P. Birmingham; 16 tr, Marie DeJohn/Publishers' Graphics; 17, Susan Goldstein; 19 t, David Lindroth Inc.; 19 cr, George Holton/Photo Researchers; 20–21 t, F. Gohier/Photo Researchers; 20 cr, Robert Frerck/Woodfin Camp; 20 bl, M. Courtney-Clarke/Photo Researchers; 21 tr, David Lindroth Inc.; 21 cl, Victor Englebert/Photo Researchers; 21 br, © Joe Viesti; 23 t, David Lindroth Inc.; 23 bl, Art Resource; 24, Larry Mulvehill/Photo Researchers; 25 both, M. Bertinetti/Photo Researchers; 27 tr, Marilyn Bass; 27 br, Melissa Hayes English/Photo Researchers; 28 cr, © Joe Viesti; 29 cl, Marilyn Bass; 32 tl, D. Thomas/Photo Researchers; 32 tr, Fred J. Maroon/Photo Researchers; 33, Paolo Koch/Photo Researchers; 34, Wally McNamee/Woodfin Camp; 35 both, U.S. Department of Agriculture; 36 tr, Tom Powers/Joseph, Mindlin & Mulvey Inc.; 36 bl, 37, and 38 both, NASA; 39 t, © 1986 Max Planck Institute for Aeronomy, Lindau/Harz, West Germany, courtesy of Dr. H.U. Keller; 39 br and inset, NASA; 40–41, NASA; 43 bl, Frank Fournier/Woodfin Camp; 45 b, Chicago Historical Society; 45 inset, David Lindroth Inc.; 46 tr, Arthur Sirdofsky; 46–47 b, Robert Frank/Melissa Turk & The Artist Network; 48, Turi MacCombie/Evelyne Johnson Associates; 49 and 50, Fiona Reid/Melissa Turk & The Artist Network; 51 tl, Harriet Phillips/Lillian Flowers, Artists' Representative; 51 br, Chuck Nicklin/Woodfin Camp; 52, Joel Snyder/Publishers' Graphics; 53, Judi Buie/Bruce Coleman Inc.; 54 all, Juan Barberis/Melissa Turk & The Artist Network; 55, © The Metropolitan Museum of Art, anonymous gift, 1981 (1981.159); 56 tr, Culver Pictures; 56 bl, Carlsbad Caverns National Park; 57 b, Arthur Sirdofsky; 57 inset, Smithsonian Institution; 58–59 t, Tom Powers/Joseph, Mindlin & Mulvey Inc.; 59 b, National Optical Astronomy Observatories; 61 t, A.N. Phelps Stokes Collection, Miriam and Ira D. Wallach Division of Art, Prints, and Photographs, The New York Public Library, Astor, Lenox and Tilden Foundations; 62, Daemmrich/Stock, Boston; 64 tl, Bettmann Archive; 64 br, Ken Ross/Viesti Associates; 65, Alvis Upitis/The Image Bank; 66–67 t, Bethlehem Steel; 66 bl, R.S. Uzzell III/Woodfin Camp; 67 tr, Fritz Henle/Photo Researchers; 68, Michael L. Abramson/Woodfin Camp; 70–71 t, Adam Woolfitt/Woodfin Camp; 70 bl, Harriet Phillips/Lillian Flowers, Artists' Representative; 71 br, Tourist Division, Georgia Department of Industry and Trade; 72, Ellis Herwig/Taurus Photos; 73 t, Michael O'Reilly/Joseph, Mindlin & Mulvey Inc.; 73 br, Tom Powers/Joseph, Mindlin & Mulvey Inc.; 74 tl, NASA Space Shuttle Mission 41G, courtesy of Technology Application Center, University of New Mexico, #41G-34-081; 75 all, Serge Labrunie/ANA/Viesti Associates; 77 tl, Dennis O'Brien/Joseph, Mindlin & Mulvey Inc.; 77 b, George Hall/Woodfin Camp; 78, The Photo Works/Photo Researchers; 79 b, Van Phillips/Leo de Wys Inc.; 79 inset, Tom McHugh/Photo Researchers; 80 bl, David Lindroth Inc.; 80 br, Mike Yamashita/Woodfin Camp; 81, Tanya Rebelo/Joseph, Mindlin & Mulvey Inc.; 82 t, Joyce Photographics/Photo Researchers; 82 inset, U.S. Department of Agriculture; 83 tr, Art Resource; 83 cr, David Lindroth Inc.; 84, NASA; 85, Tom Powers/Joseph, Mindlin & Mulvey Inc.; 86 both, National Optical Astronomy Observatories; 87 t, Tom McHugh/Photo Researchers; 87 inset, Supreme Court Historical Society; 87 br, V. Cavataio/All Sport/Woodfin Camp; 88–89, Guido Alberto Rossi/The Image Bank; 90, Michael O'Reilly/Joseph, Mindlin & Mulvey Inc.; 91 cr, Roy W. Hankey/Photo Researchers; 92, Bill Wood/Bruce Coleman Inc.; 93, Wardene Weisser/Bruce Coleman Inc.; 94, Bruce Roberts/Photo Researchers; 95, Manmade Fiber Producers Association; 96 bl, David Lindroth Inc.; 96 br, Paolo Koch/Photo Researchers.

COVER CREDITS
Center: Arthur Sirdofsky. Clockwise from top: Ken Ross/Viesti Associates; V. Cavataio/All Sport/Woodfin Camp; Adam Woolfitt/Woodfin Camp; Fiona Reid/Melissa Turk & The Artist Network; NASA; Karel A. De Gendre/ANA/Viesti Associates.

Library of Congress Catalog Card Number: 87-82741
ISBN: 0-307-70117-4

ABCDEFGHIJKLM

S *continued*

soap

Soap is a waxy substance that causes water to form suds and loosens dirt and grime.

The materials soap is made of have hardly changed in hundreds of years. Soap is made by continuously blending *tallow*—animal fat—and vegetable oils in a high-pressure tank containing boiling water. The water splits the fats into fatty acids and alcohol. The alcohol is boiled off. Sodium hydroxide—lye—is then added to the hot acids. Sodium from the lye attaches itself to one end of each fatty-acid molecule.

Soap has cleaning action because the sodium end of each molecule is attracted to water, while the fatty-acid end is attracted to oils and greases. The fatty-acid end picks up greasy dirt from the thing being washed. The sodium end allows the combination to be washed away by water.

If air is blown into the hot mixture when soap is being made, tiny bubbles of air are trapped in the soap. This kind of soap floats. If the hot liquid is sprayed up into a cold tank, it cools and falls like snow to form powdered soap.

Perfumes, colors, and other materials are usually added to soap. (*See* cosmetics.)

soccer

Soccer is the world's most popular sport. It is played in more than 140 countries, by men, women, boys, and girls. Professional soccer leagues exist in the countries of Europe, North America, South America, and Asia. Some countries have soccer leagues for players as young as four or five years old. There are also leagues for players older than 60. A good soccer game is exciting to watch. Crowds of more than 100,000 fans often attend professional soccer games.

Soccer teams from various nations compete in the World Cup games, which are held

The World Cup soccer tournament is played between national teams every four years. The winning team is world champion until the next tournament.

every four years. These championship games attract huge audiences. Millions of fans attend the games, and billions more watch the games on television. In fact, the World Cup finals are seen by more people than the Olympic Games.

How Soccer Is Played A soccer game is played by two teams of 11 players each. The object is to kick the ball into the goal of the opposing team. The game is won by the team that scores the most goals. The soccer ball is usually made of leather and is slightly smaller than a basketball. Soccer fields are most often 100 to 130 yards (91 to 119 meters) long and 50 to 100 yards (46 to 91 meters) wide. A goal net rests at each end of the field. Each goal is 24 feet (7.3 meters) wide and 8 feet (2.4 meters) high.

Players move the ball with their feet, chests, and heads. Only the *goalie*—the player who guards the team's goal—is allowed to catch the ball or touch it with the hands.

Each soccer player wears a uniform consisting of a shirt, shorts, knee socks, and special shoes. The shoes have *cleats*—short spikes—on the bottom that keep the players from slipping.

The most important skills in soccer are dribbling, passing, and shooting. Since it is illegal to touch the ball with their hands, players dribble the ball with their feet. Players also control the ball by passing it or kicking it to other team members. When the ball gets near the opponent's goal, it is time to try shooting the ball past the goalie. Good players can shoot the ball hard with their feet or their heads.

Mastering these skills takes hours of practice and teamwork. Most of the world's best soccer players learned the game as children and have had years of practice. The most famous was a Brazilian star nicknamed Pelé. Pelé began playing for Brazil's national team at the age of 16. He led Brazil to World Cup championships in 1958, 1962, and 1970.

Pelé later played for the New York Cosmos of the North American Soccer League (NASL). When Pelé played, crowds of more than 70,000 people often came to watch. After Pelé retired, many people stopped attending. A few years later, the NASL went out of business.

Still, the popularity of soccer has continued to grow in U.S. high schools and colleges. Today, more than 5,000 high schools in the U.S. have soccer teams. Many have teams for girls and for boys.

History of Soccer Games similar to soccer were played in ancient China and during the time of the Roman Empire. The game as we know it today was first played in English schools during the 1800s. It quickly spread from England to other countries. The first World Cup championship games were held in Uruguay in 1930.

A soccer field is usually longer and wider than an American football field. Players move the ball down the field without touching it with their hands.

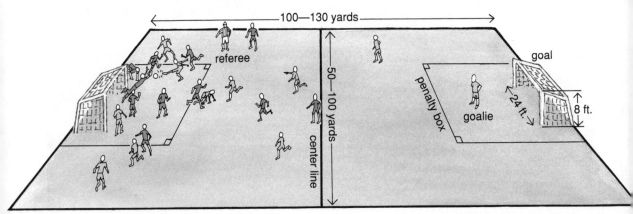

socialism

Socialism is an economic system in which the government decides what goods and services will be produced and how much they will cost. The economies of many nations are partly socialistic.

Under a socialist system, the government owns a great deal of property. It usually owns big factories, such as those that make steel. It may also own railroads, airlines, banks, and the telephone system. Often, governments in socialist countries also run public institutions such as schools and hospitals.

Socialism is different from *capitalism*, the economic system of the United States, Canada, and many other nations. In a capitalist system, almost all property is owned either by individuals or by groups of individuals. These individuals decide for themselves what goods and services to produce and how much to charge for them.

Suppose a company in a capitalist country makes bicycles. If it sells enough bicycles at a high enough price, it makes a profit. If not, the owner may decide to go out of business or to try making another product. The owner's decision is influenced by many people who buy from and sell to the company. The government does not tell the owner what to do.

Capitalism stresses freedom of choice. That is why it is also called the *free-enterprise system.* Property owners are free to make big profits if they can. They are also free to go broke.

In a socialist country, the government might decide that every worker should be able to have a bicycle. This decision—not profits—would determine whether bicycles were manufactured. If the government itself did not own the bicycle companies, it would make sure that the people who did own them would not go out of business. The government might even give the bicycle company money so that the company could keep operating.

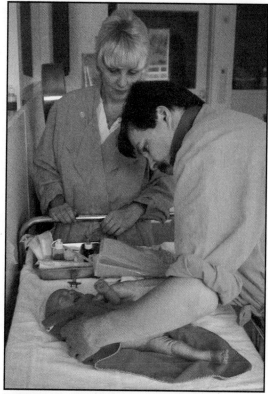

In Finland, treatment in a hospital is free to all citizens. The hospital's costs are paid from tax funds.

Socialism stresses security and equality. The government allows its citizens less economic freedom than they would have under capitalism. But it also offers many benefits, such as free education and medical care. High taxes pay for these benefits. In Sweden, one of the socialist countries of Europe, some people pay as much as four-fifths of their income in taxes.

Many great thinkers have written about socialism. The most important was a German named Karl Marx, who lived during the 1800s. Marx published his ideas in a book called *Das Kapital.*

Some of Marx's followers believe that socialism should be introduced gradually and peacefully. Today, people who hold this belief are called *socialists.* Other followers of Marx think socialism should be brought about immediately, through violence and revolution. They are called *Communists.* (*See* **communism.**)

sociology

Sociology is one of the social sciences. These are sciences that study people and how they behave. The social sciences include psychology and political science. Sociology studies how people behave in groups. Each of us is a member of several groups—a family, a class in school, a neighborhood, and an age group. People may also be grouped according to where they live and whether they are wealthy or poor.

Sociologists use various methods to study groups of people. They may prepare questions and then ask many people to answer them. They may also observe a group of people over a period of time and record everything that happens.

SOCIOLOGY

One way to understand a group of people is to divide it into smaller groups. These charts give some interesting facts about 100 students who go to Central School.

How many are boys? How many are girls?

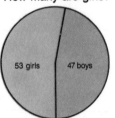

53 girls | 47 boys

What grades are they in?

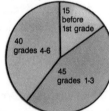

40 grades 4-6 | 15 before 1st grade | 45 grades 1-3

How do they travel to school?

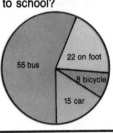

55 bus | 22 on foot | 8 bicycle | 15 car

Sociologists study groups to find out which features are shared by many groups and which features are special to just one or a few groups. They also want to know why certain groups get along well together and why others do not. Information from these studies helps us plan and build cities, neighborhoods, schools, and hospitals. Sociologists' work is especially important in cities where many groups live together.

Socrates

Socrates was a Greek philosopher and teacher who lived in the 400s B.C. He is one of the most admired men of ancient times. Although he did not leave any writings, we know about him from the writings of his most famous pupil, Plato.

Socrates lived in the city of Athens. He was a great teacher. He wanted his pupils to learn to think clearly so that they could act wisely. Socrates taught not by lecturing but by asking his students many questions. Then he would ask them to explain their answers.

Socrates had a loyal following among the Athenians. But some Athenians disliked him and did not trust his way of teaching. They thought he was encouraging young people to question things that should be accepted without any doubts.

Eventually, the leaders of Athens accused Socrates of misleading the youth of the city. After a trial, he was sentenced to death. His friends arranged for him to escape, but he refused to flee. When the time came, he calmly carried out the death sentence by swallowing poison.

A marble statue of Socrates as an old man.

Soft drinks are capped with airtight lids. Carbon dioxide gives the drink its fizz.

carbonated water (carbon dioxide + water)

flavoring + sweetener

sodium

Sodium is a soft, whitish, metallic element. It is a good conductor of electricity. Small amounts of sodium are essential to life. Our bodies absorb sodium from the *sodium chloride*—salt—in our foods. (*See* **salt**.)

In pure form, sodium burns violently if it touches air or water. So pure sodium is never found in nature. Pure sodium is made by first melting salt and then passing a strong electric current through it. This process breaks up the salt into sodium and nonmetallic chlorine. Pure sodium is used in the production of the metal titanium and in lead for gasoline. Pure sodium is also used in some electrical cables and to cool some nuclear reactors.

Most sodium is used in one of its three major compounds. *Sodium nitrate* is an important fertilizer. *Sodium hydroxide* (caustic soda) and *sodium carbonate* (soda ash) are important in many chemical processes. They are used to make glass, soaps, detergents, textiles, plastics, and other chemicals. *Baking soda,* which is made from soda ash, is used to make breads, cakes, and cookies rise.

soft drink

A soft drink is a bubbly, sweet-tasting liquid that contains no alcohol. Soft drinks are also called *soda pop, pop, soda,* and *tonic.* The name *pop* comes from the sound made when the bottle caps used in the 1800s were removed.

A soft drink is a mixture of a flavored syrup and soda water. Soda water—also called *carbonated water*—is made by adding *carbon dioxide* gas to water. The carbon dioxide forms the bubbles you see rising in your glass. Syrups are made of sugar or corn sweeteners and are flavored with fruit juices, roots, nuts, and flowers. Sometimes artificial flavors and artificial sweeteners are used.

One of the most popular soft drinks is cola, which comes from the kola nut. Ginger ale gets its flavor from gingerroot. Lemon, cherry, and orange flavorings are usually artificial. But some soft drinks contain real fruit juice.

soil

Soil is the familiar crumbly material that covers much of Earth's land. Most plants depend on soil to grow, and it is home to many burrowing animals.

How Soil Forms Soil is made of tiny particles, most of which come from rocks. The rocks are broken down by chemical changes and by *weathering*—the action of wind and water. It can take thousands of years for rocks to break down and form soil. (*See* **weathering.**)

Other particles in soil come from the breakdown of animal and plant matter. These materials form the part of soil called *humus.* Humus is usually dark. Gardeners and farmers know how important humus is to a soil. Humus provides plants with the nutrients they need for growth.

Soil Layers If you could cut deep into the ground the way you slice a cake, you would see the layers that make up soil. The soil layers are called *horizons.* The top layer, usually dark with humus, is the *topsoil.* Below it is another layer, called *subsoil.* The next layer down contains many pieces of rock and some soil similar to subsoil. Underneath is the *bedrock,* from which the soil layers probably formed. The rate at which soil forms

Soil forms in layers above the bedrock. The humus in the topsoil makes it dark.

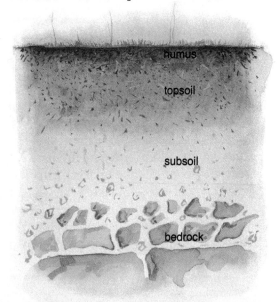

depends on the weather, climate, and the kind of rock. By examining horizons, a geologist can tell about the weathering conditions that formed the soil.

Types of Soil Soil types depend on the kind of rock particles they contain. When rock containing the mineral quartz breaks down, it forms sand particles. When rock containing silicate minerals breaks down, it forms clay particles. Clay particles are much smaller than sand particles. (*See* **clay** and **sand.**)

Most soils contain sand and clay in varying amounts. The amount of each gives a soil certain qualities. For example, soil with a great deal of clay can hold a lot of water. Soil with a great deal of sand lets water go through it easily. This quality of soil is known as its *permeability.* The more permeable the soil, the more water it allows to pass through. This is important to farmers and gardeners. Soil with too much sand lets water seep through before plant roots can absorb it. Soil with too much clay has so many small, tightly packed particles that the water gets stuck and does not pass through. The best soil for growing plants is *loam.* Loam is a crumbly soil that contains a good balance of sand and clay.

solar energy

Solar energy is energy from the sun. The sun is like a giant furnace. Its fuel is the element hydrogen. Each second, a large number of hydrogen atoms in the sun unite to form the element helium. When this happens, energy is released.

Most of that energy travels off into distant space. A small amount reaches Earth's surface. That amount is less than one-billionth of all of the sun's energy, yet it supports all life on Earth. It provides Earth with most of its light and heat. Without it, Earth would be too dark and cold for living things.

In many ways, solar energy is better than energy from oil, coal, natural gas, and wood. Earth has a limited supply of oil and other

Solar panels on the roof collect energy from the sun to provide heat and hot water. The house is also heated by a furnace, but using solar energy keeps fuel bills low.

"fossil" fuels, but solar energy is almost unlimited. Scientists expect the sun to produce energy for another 5½ billion years. Solar energy is also clean. When a fossil fuel is burned, it produces smoke and gases that pollute the air. Using solar energy does not cause air pollution. (*See* **air pollution.**)

Solar energy today is used mostly to heat homes and water. In the United States, sunlight always comes from the south. A house built with big windows facing south can be warmed by the sunlight entering the windows. Having large glass plates on the roof of a house is another way to collect the heat from sunlight. These plates also face south. Pipes containing water are beneath the plates. When the plates become hot, they heat the water. The hot water is then carried through pipes to where it can be stored or used in the house.

Certain materials called *semiconductors* can turn solar energy into electricity. These materials are made into *solar cells*. Solar cells are used to power calculators, watches, satellites, and spaceprobes. An airplane has flown the English Channel on solar energy, and cars have raced across Australia powered just by the sun.

Solar energy is available directly from the sun only while the sun is shining. So solar energy must be stored for use at night and on cloudy days. Electricity produced by solar energy can be stored in batteries. Water, too, is used to store the heat from solar energy. Heated water can stay warm for a few days.

Still, solar energy is not widely used. By the year 2000, less than 1/50 of all the energy we use will come directly from the sun.

See also **sun.**

The large square panels on this satellite collect the sun's energy, which is made into electricity to run the instruments.

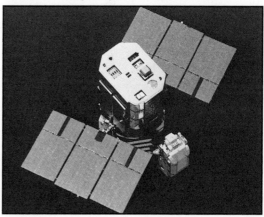

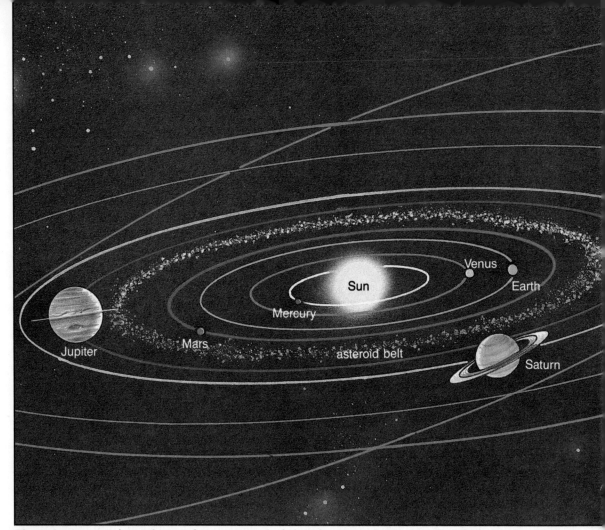

The solar system is made up of our sun and of the planets and other bodies that orbit it. Earth is the third planet out from the sun.

solar system

Our solar system is made up of our sun and all of the heavenly bodies that travel around it. These include the nine known planets, the moons circling some of the planets, asteroids, meteors, and comets. Some scientists think there may be a tenth planet, which they call Planet X.

The sun is a star at the center of the solar system. All the planets revolve around it in almost circular orbits. Each planet orbits on its own path. Mercury's orbit is closest to the sun—about 58 million kilometers (36 million miles) from it. Then come the orbits of Venus, Earth, Mars, Jupiter, Saturn, Uranus, Neptune, and Pluto. Pluto, the planet usually farthest from the sun, orbits it at an average distance of 5.8 billion kilometers (3½ billion miles).

Pluto's orbit does not mark the outer edge of our solar system. Astronomers also include a more distant region, where comets are formed. This region extends 4½ to 15 trillion kilometers (3 to 9 trillion miles) from the sun. No one has seen the region through a telescope, and no spacecraft has explored it yet. But astronomers are certain it is there.

How We Learned About the Solar System
Astronomers have not always known that planets revolve around the sun. Ancient peoples believed that the sun, planets, and stars—the whole universe—circled Earth. As early as 300 B.C., some Greek astronomers thought that the sun was the center of the universe. But few people believed this.

To us on Earth, the sun and stars appear to revolve around our planet. Even though we know better, we still say the sun "moves across the sky." Actually, it is the rotation

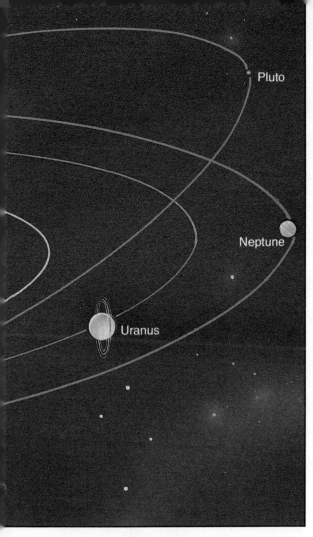

Pluto

Neptune

Uranus

the *heliocentric*—"sun-centered"—system. In 1610, through one of the first telescopes, Galileo saw four satellites orbiting Jupiter. His discovery showed that Copernicus's system was correct—everything did not revolve around Earth. At first, few people believed this. As more astronomers had the chance to view the sky through telescopes, they became convinced that Copernicus and Galileo were right. (*See* **Copernicus** and **Galileo**.)

The Solar System and the Universe Our solar system is part of a *galaxy*—a large group of stars—called the Milky Way. The Milky Way contains about 100 billion stars. The distance across the Milky Way is so great that it is measured in *light-years*. A light-year is the distance light travels in one year—almost 9.4 trillion kilometers (5.9 trillion miles). The Milky Way is 100,000 light-years across—and it is not an especially large galaxy! (*See* **Milky Way** and **galaxy**.)

Our solar system is about 32,000 light-years from the center of the galaxy. Along with the other stars in the galaxy, our sun revolves around the galaxy's center in an almost circular orbit. But it takes a long time for the sun and its system to complete one revolution—about 225 million years.

Astronomers have categories for various kinds of stars. Our sun is classified as a "yellow dwarf." This means it is about average in size and brightness. (*See* **star**.)

No one knows whether any stars besides our sun have planets or other satellites revolving around them. But some astronomers have found evidence of other systems like our solar system. In the future, better telescopes may provide more information.

The Parts of the Solar System If you could measure the *mass*—the amount of matter—in each part of the solar system, you would find that the sun has about 99 percent of the solar system's mass. Jupiter—the largest planet—and Saturn—the second-largest planet—contain almost all the remaining 1 percent. The small amount left over is divided among the other planets, their moons, asteroids, and other objects.

of Earth that makes the sun appear to travel across the sky.

Early astronomers had difficulty explaining the planets' movements across the sky. Unlike the sun, moon, and stars, the planets seemed to move in one direction for a while and then move in the opposite direction. In fact, the word *planet* means "wanderer" in Greek. Astronomers based their explanations for these movements on the idea that Earth was at the center of the universe. But their explanations were very complicated. The more they observed, the more complicated their explanations became. Despite this, most astronomers believed the Earth-centered theory for almost 1,800 years.

In 1543, the Polish astronomer Copernicus showed that the movements of the planets were easier to understand if the sun was the center of the system. His explanation became known as the Copernican system, or

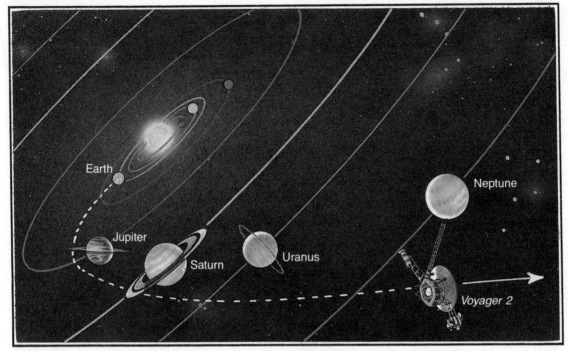

The U.S. spaceprobe *Voyager 2* was sent into space in 1977. It has sent back photographs and other information about Jupiter, Saturn, Uranus, and Neptune.

The sun's great mass creates a strong gravitational pull. In fact, the sun's gravity is so strong that it keeps all the planets, comets, and asteroids in orbit. If it were not for this gravity, the planets, comets, and asteroids would fly off into space.

The sun also provides warmth and light. Earth receives just the right amount of this heat and light for living things to survive. (*See* **sun.**)

In addition to radiating heat and light, the sun gives off what astronomers call *solar wind.* This is not the kind of wind you feel against your skin. Solar wind is a steady flow of particles given off by the sun. These particles are mostly electrons and protons—parts of atoms. They escape from the *corona*—the outermost layer of the sun. High temperatures cause the gases of the corona to expand, forcing the release of the particles. The solar system is constantly bathed in solar wind. Astronomers think the solar wind extends beyond Pluto's orbit. They also think that the solar wind is the cause of the northern lights here on Earth. (*See* **northern lights.**)

Scientists place the nine planets in two groups. The *inner planets*—Mercury, Venus, Earth, and Mars—have orbits closest to the sun. The *outer planets*—Jupiter, Saturn, Uranus, Neptune, and Pluto—have the more distant orbits. (*See* **planet.**)

All the planets revolve around the sun in the same direction—counterclockwise. But the nearer a planet's orbit is to the sun, the faster the planet travels around the sun. Mercury, the planet closest to the sun, travels at almost 48 kilometers (30 miles) per second. Pluto, the farthest away, pokes along at 4.5 kilometers (3 miles) per second.

The planets also *rotate*—spin—as they orbit the sun. All the planets except Venus and Uranus rotate counterclockwise. Venus and Uranus rotate clockwise. Uranus stands out for another reason. The other planets spin standing up straight or leaning just a bit—like a top. For some reason, Uranus has fallen over on its side. It rolls along like a ball instead of spinning like a top.

So far, scientists have discovered 61 *moons* in our solar system. A moon—also called a *satellite*—is a fairly large object that orbits a planet. Every planet except Mercury and Venus has one or more moons orbiting it. Saturn has the most moons—perhaps as many as 23. Earth has only one, but its moon is among the largest. Jupiter has the largest moon—Ganymede, which is about 5,280 kilometers (3,300 miles) in diameter. Deimos, a moon orbiting Mars, is the smallest known moon—only about 11 kilometers (7 miles) in diameter. (*See* **moon.**)

In addition to the nine major planets, thousands of tiny planets called *asteroids* orbit the sun. Most asteroids are found in the *asteroid belt*—an area between the orbits of Mars and Jupiter. The biggest asteroid, Ceres, is almost 1,000 kilometers (625 miles) in diameter. (*See* **asteroid.**)

Comets are clumps of frozen gases and dust. Astronomers think they come from the outer fringes of our solar system. They call that distant region the "Oort Cloud."

Though astronomers cannot see the Oort Cloud in their telescopes, they think it is thick with clumps of frozen gases. The clumps are believed to be in orbit around the sun. But every now and then, gravity from a passing star pulls one or more clumps out of orbit. This sends the clump heading toward the sun, and it becomes a comet. It may take tens of thousands of years, but eventually the comet closes in on the sun at the solar system's center. Then, depending on its path, the comet may crash into the sun or go into a long looping orbit around it. (*See* **comet.**)

Meteoroids are chunks of rock or iron from space that are attracted to Earth by gravity. They may come from the asteroid belt, or perhaps from the Oort Cloud. Most meteoroids burn up in Earth's atmosphere. Those that actually hit Earth are called *meteorites.* (*See* **meteors and meteorites.**)

How Long Can the Solar System Last?
Astronomers think our solar system began as a gigantic cloud of gases and dust, about 4½ billion years ago. That seems like a long time to most of us, and you may wonder how much longer our solar system can last.

Several planets have more than one moon. This is Ganymede, Jupiter's largest moon.

Astronomers estimate that the total life span of the sun will be 10 billion years. Since it is already 4½ billion years old, this means we can expect the sun to keep on shining for the next 5½ billion years.

solid

Matter is made up of molecules. It exists in three phases—solid, liquid, and gas. The molecules move differently in each phase. In a solid, the molecules are close together and move slightly. This gives a solid a definite shape and volume. In a liquid, the molecules are farther apart and move more. This makes liquids flow. The molecules in gases are even farther apart and move freely.

Metal, wood, stone, plastic, and ice are some common solids. Many solids, especially metals and minerals, form *crystals.* The atoms in a crystal are arranged in a regular, repeated three-dimensional pattern. You can actually see the shapes of some crystals. For example, salt is a cube-shaped crystal. (*See* **molecule** and **crystal.**)

If the atoms in a solid are not arranged in a regular, repeated pattern, the solid is a *glass.* The most familiar glass is found in bottles, windows, mirrors, and many other products. *Natural glass* forms when lava from a volcano cools so quickly that it does not have time to form crystals. The mineral obsidian is a natural glass.

Matter changes from one phase to another with changes in temperature. Sometimes, the temperature must rise very high or drop very low for the matter to change. When a solid is heated, some of the energy from the heat loosens the bonds between the molecules. As the bonds break, the solid usually melts and becomes a liquid. Each kind of crystal becomes a liquid at a definite temperature, called its *melting point.*

The temperature at which matter becomes a gas is called its *boiling point.* The boiling point of some matter is the same as its melting point, or lower. That is why solids such as dry ice (frozen carbon dioxide) and iodine turn directly from a solid into a gas instead of a liquid.

Glass does not have a melting point. Even as a solid, it acts like a liquid, because its molecules are already in a loose, random arrangement. As the temperature rises, solid glass becomes runny, like a thick liquid. If the temperature is raised high enough, glass changes into gas.

As a liquid cools, the bonds between the molecules become tighter, and the liquid becomes a solid.

See also **gas; liquid; matter;** and **glass.**

Some solids are soft and will bend.
Others are hard and will break or tear.

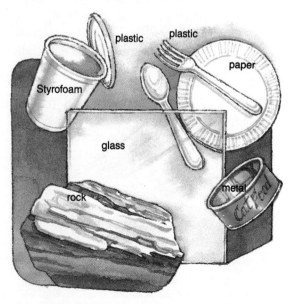

solid waste

Solid waste includes most of the things that people throw away. Food, paper, and small plastic and metal objects usually go into the trash. Solid waste also includes old cars, washing machines, televisions, and other large items that people do not want anymore. Each year, people produce millions of tons of solid waste.

Some solid waste is shipped out into the ocean and dumped overboard. Other solid waste is burned in large furnaces called *incinerators.* These reduce the waste to ash and destroy disease-causing organisms. But the ash, too, is a solid waste that must be disposed of. Often, solid waste is used as *landfill.* It is carried by truck to large holes in the ground, dumped in, and packed down. When the hole is completely filled, it is covered with earth. Houses or a park may then be built on it.

There are problems with each way of dealing with solid waste. When solid waste is burned, it gives off harmful gases. These gases add to air pollution. Ocean dumping pollutes oceans, and wastes may wash up on beaches. Landfills have different problems. Sometimes they attract rats and other animals that spread diseases. The trash may contain poisonous materials, making it unsafe for people to use the area later. There are also not enough places left where landfills can be built.

Some people dispose of solid wastes in ways that are illegal. Soft-drink cans are tossed from car windows. Old cars and refrigerators are dumped into creeks. Poisonous chemicals are buried in metal containers that rust, allowing the contents to seep into the soil and water. These acts cause solid wastes to be a problem for everyone.

One way to deal with the problem of solid waste is to *recycle* materials—use them again. Paper, aluminum cans, and glass can be recycled. So can the metal from old cars and other machines. Used paper can be shredded and made into pulp to be turned

Burning trash leaves mountains of waste (above). Materials such as old newspapers can be recycled.

into new paper. Aluminum and other metals can be melted, then reshaped into new products. Glass bottles can be cleaned and sterilized, then used again.

Using *biodegradable* materials is another solution to the problem of too much solid waste. Biodegradable materials, such as paper, can be broken down by bacteria and become part of the soil. Plastics, glass, metals, and some other solid materials are not biodegradable. Creating less waste in the first place is the best way to cut down on solid wastes.

Solomon Islands, *see* **Pacific Islands**

Somalia, *see* **Africa**

sound

Think of all the different sounds you hear each day. The sound of an alarm clock may wake you. Then you might hear familiar voices, a dog barking, water running, or music playing as you get ready for school. Once outside, you may hear the pleasant sounds of birds singing or the harsh sounds of traffic. Whether pleasant or harsh, loud or soft, all sounds have something in common. They are all caused by *vibrations*—tiny, rapid back-and-forth movements—that travel through objects or air.

How Sound Travels Sound travels in waves, and the sound waves must have a *medium*—something to travel in. Sound waves may travel through air, liquids, and solid objects. You cannot hear any sound in a *vacuum*—a place with no air, liquid, or solid.

To understand how sound waves travel, think of what happens when you throw a pebble into a still pond. Water waves spread out in circles from where the pebble hit. Sound waves act in a similar way. They spread out in circles from the source of the sound. The sound waves also must travel through something.

Scientists call sound waves *compression waves* or *longitudinal waves*. A compression wave travels only through a medium. It does this by pushing the medium's molecules close together and then letting them spring back. Over and over, the molecules move back and forth while the wave moves forward. In the water wave, the molecules move up and down while the wave moves forward.

Sound waves travel at different speeds through different mediums. They travel fastest through solids and slowest through gases. Sound is also affected by temperature. It travels faster through warmer air. In air at 0° C (32° F), sound travels at 331 meters per second (740 miles per hour). At 20° C (68° F), sound travels through air at 344 meters per second (758 miles per hour). The speed at

15

which a sound travels does not affect how it sounds to you.

Features of Sound Waves Sound waves have many features that can be measured. The *loudness* of a sound can vary, depending on your distance from its source, how well you hear, and the energy of the sound wave. Scientists call the energy of a sound wave its *amplitude.* Amplitude refers to the height of the wave. On a radio, you control the amplitude of the sound by raising or lowering the volume.

Amplitude

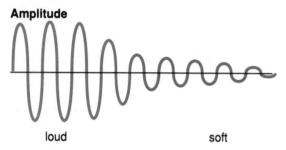

loud   soft

The *pitch* of a sound is how high or how low the sound is. Pitch is measured in *frequency*—how many times per second the sound wave vibrates. A squeaking noise or a note from a flute has a high pitch and a high frequency. A dull thud or a note from a tuba has a low pitch and a low frequency. The human ear can detect sounds with pitches ranging from as low as 15 vibrations per second to about 5,000 vibrations per second.

Pitch

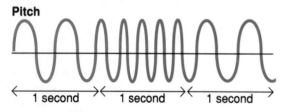

← 1 second →← 1 second →← 1 second →

The sound of middle C played on the piano has a frequency of 256 vibrations per second. Some animals, such as dogs and bats, can hear high-frequency pitches that the human ear cannot.

Another feature of sound is its *timbre*—its quality. A trumpet and a flute may be playing exactly the same pitch, but their sounds will be different because each instrument has a different timbre.

This fife and similar instruments produce high pitches and clear timbres.

Kinds of Sounds The many sources of sound and the many mediums through which sounds travel create the wide variety of sounds we hear. A piano has strings of different thicknesses and lengths. When they are struck, each one vibrates at its own rate and produces its own pitch. A trumpet player can produce different pitches by pressing down on valves. The valves change the length of the column of vibrating air inside the trumpet. This produces different pitches.

Differences in the size, thickness, and flexibility of the vocal cords make each person's voice different. The vocal cords are two tough, elastic fibers in the throat. Air passing between them makes them vibrate, producing the sounds we make when we speak or sing.

Some sounds are pleasant, usually because the sounds are in a pattern. Unpleasant sounds usually have no pattern that our ears can detect. These sounds can be harmful, especially if they are very loud.

Hearing Sounds Hearing is one of the five senses. Our ears are the organs of hearing. They pick up vibrations, and nerves carry messages about the vibrations to our brains. Our brains recognize sounds and identify where the sounds are coming from. (*See* **ear** and **hearing.**)

Our ears can recognize different pitches and are sensitive to sounds of varying loudness. The *decibel scale* is used to measure how loud sounds are. On this scale, a whisper is only 20 decibels, a telephone ring is 70 decibels, and a jet flying overhead is 140 decibels. Sounds above 120 decibels are harmful to our ears.

sound recording

Sound recording is any process of storing sound so that it may be heard later. Sound recording has been used to record music, speeches, poetry readings, and other things. The sounds in movies, videos, and television programs come from sound recordings.

Thomas Edison's phonograph—invented in 1877—was the earliest machine for recording sound. It used a needle and a foil-wrapped cylinder. Sounds made the needle *vibrate*—move back and forth rapidly. The point of the needle rested on the turning cylinder and left marks of its vibrations in the foil. When a second needle followed in the first needle's tracks, the vibrations were re-created and the sound was played back.

Another inventor, Emile Berliner, improved on Edison's machine by introducing the first phonograph records. These were zinc discs on which vibration patterns were etched as sounds were recorded. Discs were cheaper than cylinders and could be copied. Soon, cylinders were not used anymore.

Today, many sound recordings are made on strong plastic discs. These phonograph records can hold 25 minutes of sound or more on each side. Sensitive needles and microphones have made sound recording more exact. Sounds picked up in the microphone are changed to electrical signals before they become wiggles on the disc. Speakers and amplifiers, which play and strengthen the sounds, make the records sound better than ever before. This improved sound equipment is called *high-fidelity*, or *hi-fi*, because the sound it produces is accurate and clear. (*See* **amplifier.**)

Sounds are recorded on phonograph records, cassette tapes, and compact discs.

Stereophonic sound was first recorded in the 1950s. This is sound picked up by two or more microphones and recorded on separate tracks on a record. Stereophonic sound is like live sound. When played back through separate speakers, the two sound tracks are heard coming from different directions, as though from different sections of an orchestra. Quadraphonic sound is recorded from four sides. When played back, it surrounds the listener with sound.

Sound can also be recorded on magnetic tape. Most tapes today are on easy-to-use cassettes. When a singer sings into a microphone, the air vibrations are changed into electronic signals. In the tape recorder, a magnet converts the electronic signals to a magnetic pattern that represents the sounds' vibrations. The sound pattern is saved on the magnetic tape.

Musicians who work with sounds made by synthesizers and computers often use magnetic tape. This works very well, since the sounds are already in the form of electronic signals. The musicians can do more work on their compositions by changing the signals on the tape.

Magnetic tape is also used in the production of phonograph records. The sounds are recorded first on tape and then transferred to a plastic disc.

Some modern methods for recording sound are *optical systems*. In these, electrical signals are changed to light patterns. This system is often used to record sounds for motion pictures. The light patterns are stored on photographic film.

Another modern recording system uses laser light to record sounds and play them from a *compact disc*. Smaller than a phonograph record, a compact disc is made from a different kind of plastic and is coated with aluminum. It is grooved with circles very close to one another. The sound pattern is changed to a mathematical pattern. This pattern is copied onto the disc by a laser beam that burns tiny pits into the disc's circles. A weaker laser beam scans the holes to play back the sound. (*See* **laser**.)

See also **phonograph**.

Sousa, John Philip

John Philip Sousa (SOO-zuh) was an American musician and composer who became known as the "March King." His marches are often played by marching bands at parades and football games. One of them, "The Stars and Stripes Forever," may be the most popular march ever written.

Sousa was born in 1854 in Washington, D.C. He played in orchestras and bands as a teenager. He began writing music, and wrote many popular light operas. A light opera was a kind of musical comedy.

When he was 26, Sousa was asked to lead the United States Marine Band. He wrote marches for the band and took it on tour to many parts of the country. Band music was very popular, and soon Sousa was the most famous band director in the country.

In 1892, Sousa left the marine band and formed his own band. The Sousa band toured the United States and many other parts of the world. Sousa made his brilliant, exciting music popular wherever the band played. In 1917, when the United States entered World War I, Sousa became bandmaster for the U.S. Navy. He died in 1932.

South Africa

Capitals: Cape Town, Pretoria, and Bloemfontein
Area: 471,443 square miles (1,221,037 square kilometers)
Population (1985): about 32,465,000
Official languages: Afrikaans, English

South Africa is a country at the southern tip of the continent of Africa. It is the richest country in Africa, with modern cities, offices, factories, and mines.

South Africa is also a troubled country. About 81 out of every 100 South Africans are black or people of mixed color. They have very few rights and cannot help choose their government. White South Africans—about 19 of every 100 people in the nation—hold nearly all the power and wealth. Black people, supported by many African nations, want more power in South Africa.

Land South Africa has about three times as much land as California. At its widest point, it extends nearly 1,000 miles (1,600 kilometers) from east to west. Most of the country has a mild, sunny climate. There is also a long ocean coastline. Some of the best farmland is along the coast. The main crops are bananas, citrus, and other fruits, sugarcane, and vegetables.

Inland, there is a huge plateau. The plateau receives little rain in most years, but parts of it are good for farming and ranching. Farmers grow wheat and wine grapes. In the northeast, there is a section called the Rand that has one of the world's largest gold deposits. South Africa mines more gold and diamonds than any other country. Other products of South Africa include chemicals, metal, clothing, and processed food.

People South African laws and customs enforce a social policy called *apartheid* (ah-PAR-tate). Apartheid means "apartness."

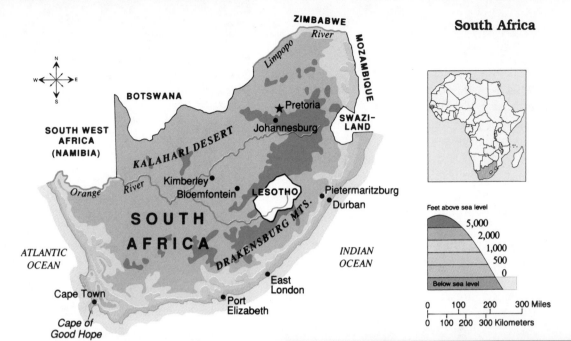

A beach near Cape Town, South Africa's largest city and one of its capitals.

The country's people are classified by the color of their skins—black, white, colored, and Asian. Each group must live according to a different set of laws and regulations. They must live in separate communities and must attend separate schools. Almost all important jobs are held by whites.

Blacks make up about two-thirds of the population. The government has set aside ten areas, called *homelands,* for black people. Each homeland is for a large tribe or group of tribes. The largest are the Xhosa and the Zulu. In the homelands, blacks lead simple, traditional lives. They live in huts with straw roofs and try to raise enough food for their families.

About half of South Africa's blacks do not live in the homelands. They live in black townships near cities, farming areas, or mines, where they work. They must carry special passes, which are checked whenever they enter or leave a white area.

Most whites in South Africa live in or near large cities. They live in houses or apartments much like those in the United States. Many of them own cars and enjoy many of the same hobbies and sports as Europeans and Americans.

More than half of the whites in South Africa are *Afrikaaners*—people whose ancestors came to South Africa from the Netherlands, Germany, and France. Their language, Afrikaans, is closely related to Dutch. The ancestors of most of the other whites came to South Africa from Britain and other English-speaking countries. They speak English.

Most Asians came to South Africa from India. "Coloreds" are people of mixed ancestry. Many of them work as servants in the homes and shops of white people. About 10 of every 100 South Africans are classified as Asian or colored. They have fewer rights than the whites do, but more than blacks.

19

History The black Africans who live in what is now South Africa came to the region at least 1,000 years ago. They formed many different tribes, each with its own language and traditions.

In the 1600s, Dutch trading companies came to the region. Some of their workers stayed and became farmers in the area around Cape Town. These people are the ancestors of today's Afrikaaners.

In 1814, the Netherlands gave control of South Africa to Britain. Soon, thousands of immigrants were coming from English-speaking lands. During the 1800s and early 1900s, there were many wars between the British and the Afrikaaners over who should rule. The British finally won. The British also conquered black African tribes in the region. They drove blacks away from the richest farmland and from places where gold and other valuable resources were found.

South Africa became independent in 1931. Soon afterward, the National party gained control of the country's affairs. The party established most of the laws of apartheid.

Black leaders in South Africa and many people in other countries around the world have protested against apartheid. They want all the people of South Africa to have the same rights. They hope that changes will come peacefully, but are afraid that apartheid may lead to civil war.

A squatter camp. By South African law, blacks must live separate from whites.

South America

South America is the fourth-largest of the world's seven continents. It is about twice the size of the United States. South America is a land of great contrasts. The world's second-highest mountain range, the Andes, rises above vast rain forests and open plains. At least five cities in South America are home to more than 4 million people. Yet about half of the continent's land is undeveloped wilderness.

Land The Atlantic Ocean is on South America's east coast, and the Pacific is on its west coast. Off the northern coast are the Caribbean Sea—an arm of the Atlantic—and the islands of the West Indies. South America connects with Central America in the northwest.

In the far south, the continent comes to a narrow point called Cape Horn. The Atlantic

At top, the Andes,
South America's long
mountain range.
Far left, people of
the Andes use llamas
to carry goods.
Left, sheep in the
plains of Patagonia.
Below, a rain forest
in the Amazon Basin.

and the Pacific meet there. Early sailors feared the high waves and terrible storms of Cape Horn. But the fog and storms in the Strait of Magellan were even worse. The Strait of Magellan cuts across the southern tip of South America.

Moving north, the land widens slowly. In the west along the Pacific coast, there are hundreds of mountainous islands. They belong to the nation of Chile and are the beginning of the Andes Mountains. The Andes extend for more than 3,000 miles (4,800 kilometers) along the Pacific shore of South America.

Only the Himalayas of Asia are higher than the Andes. More than 50 peaks in the Andes are more than 20,000 feet (6,000 meters) above sea level. Mount Aconcagua (ah-cone-KAH-gwah), at 22,834 feet (6,964 meters) above sea level, is the highest mountain in the Americas.

SOUTH AMERICAN COUNTRIES AND TERRITORIES

Country	Capital	Square Miles	Square Kilometers	Population
Argentina	Buenos Aires	1,068,297	2,766,889	30,708,000
Bolivia	La Paz; Sucre	424,162	1,098,580	6,195,000
Brazil	Brasilia	3,286,472	8,511,962	139,774,000
Chile	Santiago	292,257	756,946	12,042,000
Colombia	Bogota	439,735	1,138,914	29,347,000
Ecuador	Quito	109,483	283,561	9,378,000
*Falkland Islands	Stanley	4,700	12,173	2,000
**French Guiana	Cayenne	35,135	91,000	91,000
Guyana	Georgetown	83,000	214,970	768,000
Paraguay	Asuncion	157,047	406,752	3,989,000
Peru	Lima	496,222	1,285,215	19,698,000
Suriname	Paramaribo	63,037	163,266	375,000
Uruguay	Montevideo	68,037	176,216	2,936,000
Venezuela	Caracas	352,143	912,050	17,317,000
TOTAL		6,879,727	17,818,494	272,620,000

* A territory of the United Kingdom
** A territory of France

Between the Andes and the Pacific is Chile—the world's longest and narrowest country. It stretches more than 2,500 miles (4,000 kilometers) from north to south, but is rarely wider than 200 miles (320 kilometers) from east to west. Chile has some of South America's most productive farmland.

East of the Andes, as the continent widens, is Patagonia, a cold desert plain. Only a few hardy sheepherders live there.

North of Patagonia is the *Pampa*—a Spanish word for "grassland." Like the Great Plains of North America, the Pampa is good for cattle ranching and farming. This is the land of the *gaucho*—the South American cowboy.

East of the Pampa, reaching toward the Atlantic Ocean, is the Rio de la Plata, a giant bay into which many rivers empty. Along the Rio de la Plata are the important cities of Buenos Aires and Montevideo.

Moving north from the Pampa, you cross a region of tangled wilderness that makes up northern Argentina, Paraguay, and southern Brazil. Along the Atlantic, there is a productive farm region. In the middle of it are two big cities. One is Rio de Janeiro. The other, Sao Paulo, may be the world's largest city.

Still farther north, the continent becomes as wide as the United States. This huge bulge is covered by the Amazon River Basin.

The Amazon and the smaller rivers that empty into it drain one-third of South America—2½ million square miles (6.5 million square kilometers). (*See* **Amazon River**.)

Most of the Amazon Basin is covered by dense tropical rain forest. This forest is home to tens of thousands of animals, including colorful birds and insects. There are many kinds of monkeys, and snakes such as the tree-climbing anaconda, which may grow to more than 30 feet (6 meters). Flesh-eating piranhas live in the waters of the Amazon. In fact, about one-fourth of the known kinds of animals in the world live in South America, mostly in the Amazon Basin.

To the west of the Amazon Basin are Peru and Ecuador, mountain countries that stretch from the Andes down to the Pacific.

Moving north from the Amazon Basin, the continent begins to narrow once again. In this hot, damp region, the continent looks northward to the Atlantic Ocean and the Caribbean Sea.

South America has many natural resources. The early explorers searched for gold and silver. These metals are still mined in South America, but other minerals are now more important. Chile has large deposits of copper and of nitrate, which are used in many chemical industries. Venezuela is one of the world's leading oil-producers.

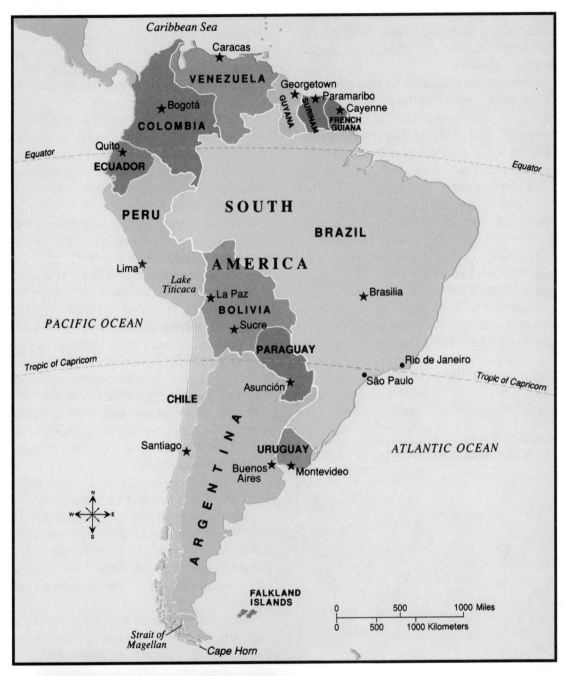

Caribbean Sea

Caracas

VENEZUELA

Georgetown
Paramaribo
GUYANA
SURINAM
Cayenne
FRENCH
GUIANA

Bogotá

COLOMBIA

Equator

Quito

ECUADOR

Equator

PERU

SOUTH

BRAZIL

Lima

AMERICA

Lake
Titicaca

La Paz

Brasilia

BOLIVIA

PACIFIC OCEAN

Sucre

PARAGUAY

Tropic of Capricorn

Rio de Janeiro

Asunción

São Paulo

Tropic of Capricorn

CHILE

ATLANTIC OCEAN

Santiago

URUGUAY

Buenos
Aires

Montevideo

A R G E N T I N A

N
W E
S

FALKLAND
ISLANDS

| 0 | | 500 | | 1000 Miles |

| 0 | 500 | | 1000 Kilometers |

Strait of
Magellan

Cape Horn

This gold mask was made by the Inca,
who once ruled an empire
in South America.

About nine-tenths of the world's emeralds come from Colombia. South America also has large amounts of metals, such as zinc, iron, and bauxite.

Timber is another natural resource. Most of the northern half of the continent is covered by tropical forests. Little of the timber is harvested. But the rain forests are threatened by poor farming practices and other human activities.

History Around the year 1500, there were more than 30 million American Indians living on the continent. Some were hunters and gatherers. Others had advanced civilizations. The Inca, who controlled Peru and Ecuador, had one of the most advanced civilizations in the world. (*See* **Inca.**)

Beginning in the 1490s, South America was explored and conquered by the Spanish and Portuguese. Early explorers were looking for riches to take home. But soon people began to settle along the shores.

According to an agreement between Spain and Portugal, Spain received control of the

A square in Buenos Aires, Argentina. The white building was once the city hall.

western part of South America, while Portugal had the right to the eastern shores. As a result, Spanish became the main language in most of South America. But in the region settled by the Portuguese—now Brazil—the official language is Portuguese.

Britain, France, and the Netherlands settled small areas along South America's northern shore. British Guiana and Dutch Guiana became the independent countries of Guyana and Suriname. French Guiana is still a territory of France.

South Americans lived under the rule of European countries until the early 1800s. Between 1800 and 1820, many wars of independence were fought, and most of today's South American countries were born. (*See* **Bolívar, Simón.**)

Many countries in South America have had violent civil wars. Small groups of rich landowners have usually controlled the governments. Today, military officers are often the most powerful government officials.

People The Indians had lived in South America for centuries before Europeans arrived. After that, many of them died of battle wounds or of diseases brought by the Europeans. Others retreated into the mountains and rain forests to avoid European control.

Today, about 30 million Indians live in South America—the same number as when the explorers arrived. In Peru, Ecuador, and Bolivia, people of Indian descent are the largest group. On the rest of the continent, Indians are a minority.

Most of the people of Argentina, Uruguay, and Brazil are descendants of Europeans. Their ancestors came from Spain, Portugal, Italy, Germany, and other countries in Europe. *Mestizos*—people of both European and Indian ancestry—are the largest group in Chile, Bolivia, and Venezuela.

Blacks of African descent are a small minority in most of South America. The largest number live in Brazil. Since the 1940s, many Asians have moved to South America. More than a million people of Japanese descent live in Brazil.

Brazil is the largest of South America's 12 countries. It covers half of South America and has about half of the continent's people. The next-largest countries are Argentina and Peru.

In 1900, nearly all South Americans lived in the countryside and worked on farms or ranches. But more and more people have moved to cities to find jobs and better living conditions. Today, more than half of all South Americans live in cities. Two of the largest cities are São Paulo and Rio de Janeiro, in Brazil. Others are Bogotá, Colombia; Lima, Peru; and Santiago, Chile.

About two of every five South Americans live on farms and ranches. Many large farms and ranches are owned by rich families and worked by hundreds of poor peasant farmers. A few plantations in Brazil are larger than some states in the United States. Coffee beans, bananas, cotton, grains, and fruits are the most important crops.

Other farms are so small that farmers can hardly grow enough food to support their own families. Many farmers still work the land by hand, using simple tools. Most are very poor. Yet the few large plantation owners are very rich and control large tracts of land. The governments of several countries are trying to divide some of the large plantations and ranches among small farmers.

See also **Argentina; Brazil; Chile; Colombia; Peru;** and **Venezuela.**

At left, music students play an instrument called the *charrango.*
Below, market day in La Paz, Bolivia.

South Carolina

Capital: Columbia
Area: 31,113 square miles (80,583 square kilometers) (40th-largest state)
Population (1980): 3,122,717 (1985): about 3,347,000 (24th-largest state)
Became a state: May 23, 1788 (8th state)

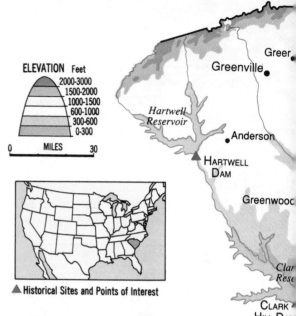

ELEVATION Feet
2000-3000
1500-2000
1000-1500
600-1000
300-600
0-300

0   MILES   30

Greer
Greenville
Hartwell Reservoir
Anderson
HARTWELL DAM
Greenwood
Clar Rese
CLARK HILL DAM

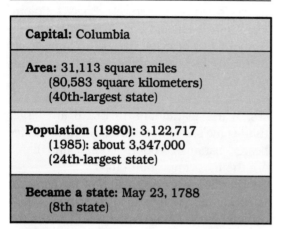

▲ Historical Sites and Points of Interest

South Carolina is a small state in the southeastern United States. It is bordered on the north by North Carolina and on the southeast by Georgia. To the east and south, it faces the Atlantic Ocean.

Land A lowland called the *Atlantic coastal plain* extends inland from the ocean for about 100 miles (161 kilometers). North of this plain is the Piedmont—an area of hills. The Blue Ridge Mountains cover the northwestern part of the state.

South Carolina has cool winters, hot summers, and a good amount of rain. Forests cover about two-thirds of the state. South Carolina's fertile soil supports thousands of farms. Most farms are on the coastal plain—the "lowlands." Along the Atlantic coast are beaches, marshes, and swamps.

An important feature of the geography of South Carolina is the *fall line.* This is an area about halfway across the state where rivers drop from the Piedmont to the coastal plain. Waterfalls along the fall line have long been used as a source of power.

History Cherokee, Sioux, and many other Indian groups once lived in South Carolina. The Spanish and French tried to establish settlements there during the 1500s. The first settlement to succeed was founded at Albemarle Point in 1670 by a group of Englishmen. Ten years later, the settlement was moved to nearby Charles Towne—today's Charleston.

Charleston was in the province of Carolina, which had been named in honor of King Charles I of England. In 1730, Carolina was divided into two separate royal colonies—North Carolina and South Carolina. During the Revolutionary War, battles fought on South Carolina soil kept the southern colonies from being controlled by the British. South Carolina's Andrew Pickens and Francis Marion—known as "Swamp Fox"—were Revolutionary War heroes.

Cotton became the state's chief crop after the cotton gin was invented in 1793. Many black slaves were brought from Africa to work on large farms called *plantations.* When Abraham Lincoln was elected president in 1860, many South Carolinians thought slavery would become illegal. That same year, South Carolina became the first state to *secede*—withdraw—from the Union. Other southern states followed.

The Civil War broke out on April 12, 1861, when Confederate troops fired on Union troops at Fort Sumter, in the harbor at Charleston. Thousands of South Carolinians were killed in the Civil War, and many plantations and businesses were destroyed. After his famous "march to the sea" in Georgia, General William T. Sherman took his Union army north through the Carolinas. South Carolina was left broken and bitter. In 1868, three difficult years after the end of the war, South Carolina rejoined the Union.

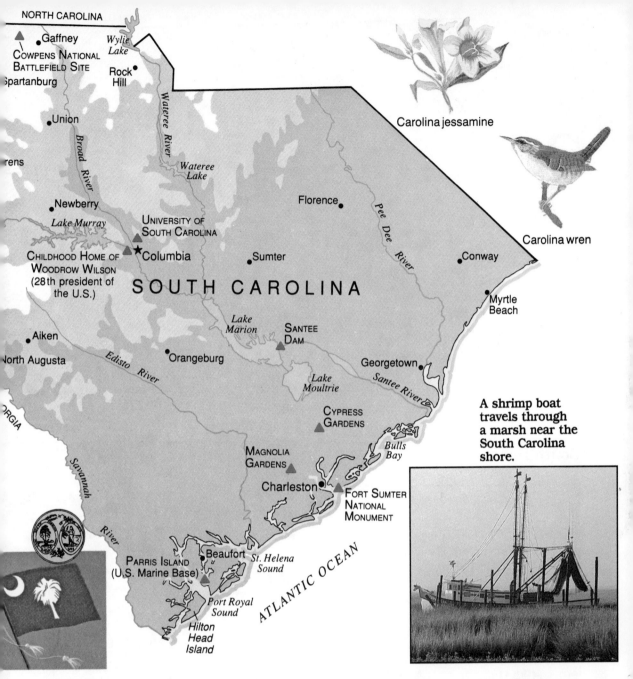

NORTH CAROLINA

Gaffney
COWPENS NATIONAL
BATTLEFIELD SITE
Spartanburg

Wylie
Lake

Rock
Hill

Union

Broad River

Wateree River

ⁿrens

Newberry

Lake Murray

UNIVERSITY OF
SOUTH CAROLINA

CHILDHOOD HOME OF
WOODROW WILSON
(28th president of
the U.S.)

★ Columbia

Wateree
Lake

Florence

Pee Dee River

Sumter

Conway

SOUTH CAROLINA

Myrtle
Beach

Aiken

North Augusta

Edisto River

Orangeburg

Lake
Marion

SANTEE
DAM

Lake
Moultrie

Georgetown

Santee River

Carolina jessamine

Carolina wren

CYPRESS
GARDENS

MAGNOLIA
GARDENS

Bulls
Bay

A shrimp boat
travels through
a marsh near the
South Carolina
shore.

Charleston

FORT SUMTER
NATIONAL
MONUMENT

Savannah

ⁿRGIA

River

PARRIS ISLAND
(U.S. Marine Base)

Beaufort

St. Helena
Sound

ATLANTIC OCEAN

Port Royal
Sound

Hilton
Head
Island

People Over half of South Carolina's people live in farm areas. South Carolina grows more peaches than any other state except California, and it is fourth among the states in tobacco production. Other farm products include soybeans, peanuts, and poultry.

Today, manufacturing is more important to the state's economy than agriculture. Many factories make *textiles*—yarns and fabrics of cotton, wool, polyester, and silk. South Carolina leads all other states in the production of *finished cloth*—cloth that has been dyed or printed. Factories in South

Carolina also produce lumber, paper products, electrical equipment, and glass. Tourism is also part of the state's economy. There are many resorts in the Blue Ridge Mountains and along the Atlantic shore.

Columbia is the capital and largest city of South Carolina. It is a center of government and manufacturing.

Charleston is a busy seaport. The city's magnificent gardens draw many tourists. So do the homes of the historic harbor area. The Charleston Museum, which opened in 1733, is one of the oldest museums in the country.

27

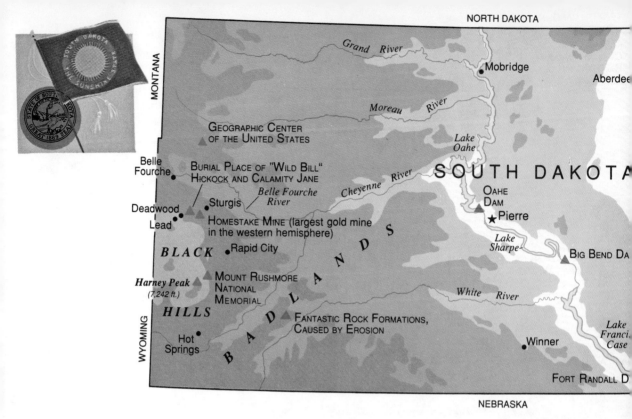

NORTH DAKOTA

MONTANA

Grand River

Mobridge

Aberdee

Moreau River

GEOGRAPHIC CENTER
OF THE UNITED STATES

Lake
Oahe

SOUTH DAKOTA

Belle
Fourche

BURIAL PLACE OF "WILD BILL"
HICKOCK AND CALAMITY JANE

Cheyenne River

OAHE
DAM

*Belle Fourche
River*

Deadwood

Sturgis

★ Pierre

Lead

HOMESTAKE MINE (largest gold mine
in the western hemisphere)

Lake
Sharpe

BIG BEND DA

BLACK

Rapid City

B A D L A N D S

Harney Peak
(7,242 ft.)

MOUNT RUSHMORE
NATIONAL
MEMORIAL

White River

HILLS

FANTASTIC ROCK FORMATIONS,
CAUSED BY EROSION

Lake
Franci
Case

Hot
Springs

Winner

FORT RANDALL D

NEBRASKA

South Dakota

Capital: Pierre	
Area: 77,116 square miles (199,730 square kilometers) (16th-largest state)	
Population (1980): 690,768 (1985): about 708,000 (45th-largest state)	
Became a state: November 2, 1889 (40th state)	

A herd of bison (American buffalo)
roam through western South Dakota.

South Dakota, the "Sunshine State," lies in the north-central United States. Each year, millions of people visit South Dakota's Mount Rushmore National Memorial, where the faces of four U.S. presidents have been carved. (*See* **Rushmore, Mount.**)

Land Summers are hot and winters are cold in South Dakota. The state gets about 20 inches (50.8 centimeters) of rain every year.

The Missouri River flows south through the state, then turns east to form part of the

border with Nebraska. Rolling *prairies* —grasslands—lie east of the Missouri. Grains grow well in the rich prairie soil. South Dakota produces more oats and rye than any other state. Other crops include wheat and barley. (*See* **Missouri River.**)

The land is higher and has more hills west of the Missouri River. The soil is not good for farming, but it is excellent pastureland for animals to graze on. Beef cattle, sheep, and hogs are raised on large farms and ranches in this part of the state.

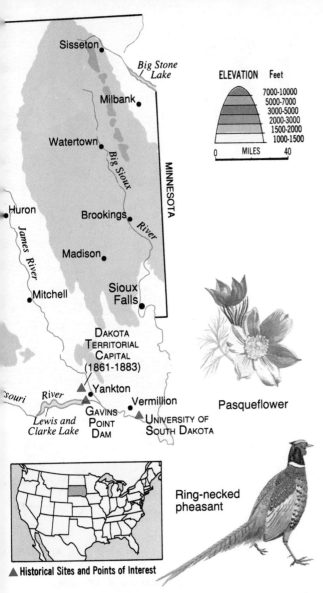

ELEVATION Feet

7000-10000
5000-7000
3000-5000
2000-3000
1500-2000
1000-1500

0   MILES   40

Pasqueflower

Ring-necked
pheasant

▲ Historical Sites and Points of Interest

in 1803 as part of the Louisiana Purchase. The following year, Meriwether Lewis and William Clark came up the Missouri River to explore the new U.S. lands. Their reports about the great number of fur-bearing animals brought many trappers and traders to the area. (*See* **Louisiana Purchase** and **Lewis and Clark Expedition.**)

Even more settlers arrived when steamboats began to travel the Missouri River. So many came that by 1855 there were almost no fur-bearing animals left. At about that time, the Indians allowed settlers onto their lands. The Dakota Territory was organized in 1861. It originally included South Dakota and parts of North Dakota, Wyoming, and Montana.

In 1874, gold was discovered in the Black Hills. This area was west of the Missouri River. It belonged to the Sioux and was sacred to them. When large numbers of miners came looking for gold, the Sioux were outraged. Led by Sitting Bull and Crazy Horse, the Sioux tried to drive the settlers away. Army troops were called in, and there were many fierce battles. One of these, "Custer's Last Stand," took place in neighboring Montana. (*See* **Custer, George Armstrong** and **Sitting Bull.**)

The Indians signed a treaty in 1876 that forced them to give up their claims to the Black Hills. Most of the Sioux moved west of the Missouri River, to *reservations*—lands set aside by the government for the Indians. Shortly afterward, railroad service from the East extended across the area. The population grew so rapidly that South Dakota became a state in 1889.

People South Dakota has more land set aside for Indians than any other state except Arizona. Almost 50,000 Indians live on or near the state's nine reservations. They grow crops and raise livestock. Most South Dakotans work as farmers, ranchers, or miners. There are few factories and no very large cities. Most of the people live on farms or in small towns. Pierre is the capital of South Dakota. Sioux Falls is the largest city.

The Badlands lie in the southwestern part of South Dakota. This is an area where wind and water have *eroded*—worn away—the land and left strangely shaped hills, rock towers, cliffs, and deep gullies. Few plants grow there. (*See* **Badlands.**)

The Black Hills are to the west of the Badlands. Called the "richest hundred square miles on earth," the Black Hills contain deposits of almost every precious mineral known. The Homestake Gold Mine, near the town of Lead, is the top-producing gold mine in the United States.

History In the language of the Sioux Indians, the word *dakota* means "friend." The Sioux, Cheyenne, and Arikara Indians lived in the region before Europeans arrived. The United States bought the area from France

South Korea, *see* Korea

South Pole

Where can you stand so a step in any direction will be a step to the north? The only place where this is possible is the South Pole—the southernmost place on Earth.

Think of a giant line running through the center of the earth. One end comes out at the North Pole. The other end comes out at the South Pole. This imaginary line is the earth's *axis.* The earth makes a full turn on its axis each day.

On a map, you can locate the South Pole by looking for the lines of *longitude*—the lines drawn from north to south on the map. All the lines of longitude meet at the South Pole and the North Pole. They are farthest apart at the equator. This imaginary line goes around the middle of the earth, halfway between the Poles.

Another way to find the South Pole is to look for Antarctica, the world's fifth-largest continent. The South Pole is located near the center of Antarctica. (*See* **Antarctica.**)

Winter temperatures at the South Pole average −70° F (−56.1° C). Even in summer, temperatures there rarely rise above 0° F (−17.6° C). Summer at the South Pole begins around December 21 and lasts until about March 21.

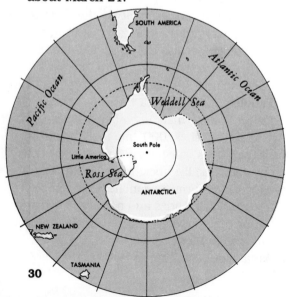

The extreme cold makes travel difficult. In the early 1900s, two groups of explorers raced to be the first to reach the South Pole. One group, led by Roald Amundsen, of Norway, used sled dogs and skis. They reached the South Pole in December 1911 and planted a flag there. (*See* **Amundsen, Roald.**)

The other team, led by Robert Scott, of Britain, used ponies to carry heavy loads. But the ponies died of the cold, and the men had to carry everything on foot. They reached the South Pole in January 1912, and found Amundsen's flag already there.

Scott's group hurried to reach their ships again. But the men were very tired, and food was running out. The weather grew even colder, and blizzards set in. Scott and his men froze to death before they could reach safety. (*See* **Scott, Robert.**)

See also **North Pole.**

ARCTIC OCEAN

NEW SIBERIAN ISLANDS

East Siberian Sea

Bering Sea

Novaya Zemlya

Severnaya Zemlya

Laptev Sea

urents Sea

Kara Sea

Lena River

VERKHOYANSK RANGE

Kamchatka Peninsula

Sea of Okhotsk

S i b e r i a

Yakutsk

Aldan River

Ob River

Yenisei

SOVIET UNION

erdlovsk

helyabinsk

Omsk

Krasnoyarsk

River

Angara River

Lake Baikal

Sakhalin

Tatar Strait

KURIL ISLANDS

PACIFIC OCEAN

Novosibirsk

Irkutsk

Ulan-Ude

Khabarovsk

CHINA

raganda

Lake Balkhash

CHINA

MONGOLIA

Vladivostok

N
W   E
S

Alma-Ata

Issyk-Kul

ELEVATION Feet

Over 10000
5000- 10000
2000- 5000
1000- 2000
0- 1000
Below sea level

0   Miles   600

Soviet Union

Capital: Moscow
Area: 8,649,496 square miles (22,402,194 square kilometers)
Population (1985): about 277,504,000
Official language: Russian

The Soviet Union is the largest country in the world. It has more land than all of Canada, the United States, and Mexico combined! From east to west, the Soviet Union stretches across 11 of the world's 24 time zones. When it is noon in the far western part of this vast country, it is 11 at night on its eastern border.

People are scattered across this huge land. The country has the third-largest population in the world, after China and India. It has about as many people as the United States and Canada combined.

In English, the official name of this nation is the Union of Soviet Socialist Republics. This name is often abbreviated to USSR. The republics of the Soviet Union are something like states in the United States, or provinces in Canada.

Land About one-fourth of the Soviet Union is in Europe. The rest is in Asia. About two-thirds of the country's people live in the European region, which has large cities and heavy industry. It also has most of the country's rich farmland. Among the most important crops are grains, potatoes, sugar beets, and other vegetables. Each year, Soviet farmers are among the world's top three producers of wheat, potatoes, meat, and sugar.

The Ural Mountains run north and south between the European and Asian parts of

Left, a village at the foot of the Caucasus Mountains. Right, the Winter Palace in Leningrad, once the winter home of the czars and now an art museum.

the nation. Soviet Asia extends east from the Urals to the Pacific Ocean. Much of it is the huge region called Siberia. Northern Siberia is so cold and barren that few people live there. The eastern tip of Siberia reaches to within a few miles of Alaska. (*See* **Siberia.**)

The Soviet Union has thousands of miles of coastline, but only a few major ports. In the far west, facing Scandinavia, is the port of Leningrad on the Baltic Sea. The port of Odessa is on the Black Sea, in the south. Ships can travel from the Black Sea into the Mediterranean. On the Pacific coast, facing Japan, there is the port of Vladivostok. The long Soviet shoreline on the Arctic Ocean is frozen for part of the year.

No country is richer in natural resources than the Soviet Union. It is the world's leading oil producer and has one-fourth of the world's reserves of timber. Siberia and the Ural Mountains have coal and iron ore.

People The Soviet Union is made up of 15 republics. Each is a different size—in land and in number of people. The largest is the Russian Federated Republic. It stretches from the Baltic Sea in the west to the Pacific Ocean in the east and has about three-fourths of the country's land. It also has about half of the Soviet Union's people,

and includes the major cities of Moscow, Leningrad, and Gorki.

Most of the people living in the Russian Federated Republic are of Russian descent. Their language, Russian, is the official language of the Soviet Union, even though more than 100 other languages are spoken across the nation.

The Ukrainian Republic takes up the southern part of Soviet Europe. It has about twice as many people as California. Its largest cities are Kiev and Kharkov. The Ukraine is known as the "breadbasket" of the Soviet Union, because its farms produce wheat and many other crops.

Other, smaller republics cluster around the western and southern edges of the Soviet Union. Three of them in the west—the Lithuanian, Latvian, and Estonian republics—were once independent countries.

People in the southern and eastern republics are related to Asian peoples. The Tajik, for example, are a mountain people related to the Asian peoples of neighboring Iran and Afghanistan.

The Soviet Union is the most important and powerful communist country in the world. Its government keeps tight control over the way people work and live.

These students in an elementary school in Siberia are studying arithmetic.

To understand the Soviet government, it helps to understand how it is different from governments in the United States, Canada, and western Europe. In these countries, a person or family can own a home. Individuals can also own a business or factory. Businesses compete with each other to make the best goods at the lowest prices. A person who does not like a job can look for another one. People can move from one region or home to another.

In the Soviet Union, the government owns almost all property and businesses. Nearly everyone works for the government. The government decides where most people will live, assigns them to jobs, and sets their wages. It also sets prices for most goods.

At the same time, the Soviet government provides many services to its people. For example, all schools and medical care are free. Houses and apartments are owned by the government and are inexpensive to rent.

In return, the government expects people to live according to strict rules. They are required to support their government. They are discouraged from practicing any religion. Yet many people continue to do so in secret.

The government also controls the radio and television stations and all publishers of newspapers, magazines, and books. Government officials decide what news and opinions people should hear and read. Protests against the government are not allowed.

People who break the rules risk losing their jobs or being sent to jail. People who protest against the government or have unpopular views may be sent to prison camps in Siberia.

People in Soviet cities live in government apartment buildings. But good housing is scarce. A family may have to share a small apartment with another family. Few Soviet families own a car, and many do not have a telephone in their home.

In the countryside, there are large *collective farms*—farms that are owned by the government. Some farmworkers may keep private gardens to raise some food for their own families. People who live in the countryside have even fewer conveniences than do people in the cities.

History During its early history, there were many small states in the land that is now the Soviet Union. The first Russian state grew up around what is now the city of Kiev in the 800s.

In the 1200s, Mongol warriors from the East swept into Russia and conquered the peoples there. They controlled the region for 250 years. Finally, Ivan III of Moscow—called Ivan the Great—gained the support of several states in Russia. He refused to pay taxes to the Mongols and ended their control.

The rulers who followed Ivan were known as *czars*. In the early 1600s, after a time of civil war and invasion, Michael Romanov became the czar. His family ruled Russia for the next 300 years. Gradually, Russia grew more powerful and took over new territories.

Peter the Great ruled in the early 1700s. He brought new ideas from Europe and made Russia an important power in Europe. He built a new city called St. Petersburg on the Baltic Sea. Today, that city is named Leningrad.

In 1812, the French conqueror Napoleon led his army into Russia. He hoped to add it

The day the Communist Party took power is celebrated on November 7. For the holiday, Red Square in Moscow is decorated with the Soviet flag and a picture of Lenin.

to his empire. He occupied Moscow, but the French army was forced to retreat when winter set in. The Russians attacked the retreating army and destroyed food supplies. The French army was destroyed, and Russia was safe once again. (*See* **Napoleon.**)

Following ancient customs, landowners in Russia kept peasant workers almost as slaves. These workers were called *serfs.* But in 1861, under strong pressure for reform, Czar Alexander II freed the serfs.

The late 1800s were a golden age for Russia. Great novels written at this time by Dostoyevsky and Tolstoy are still read and admired around the world. The music of Tchaikovsky and other Russian composers is still played.

At the same time, many people were asking for more changes in Russia. The czars became weak, and people wanted a new kind of government. In 1917, Russia was being defeated by Germany in World War I. Political leaders revolted and killed the czar and his family.

At first, there was a democratic government. Then V. I. Lenin and his Bolshevik party seized power. The Bolsheviks believed in the communist economic and political ideas of Karl Marx. Lenin gradually got rid of all his opponents. In 1922, he renamed the country. It became the Union of Soviet Socialist Republics. (*See* **Russian Revolution** and **Lenin, V. I.**)

After Lenin died in 1924, Joseph Stalin took over. Stalin became a powerful dictator. During his rule, the Soviet Union grew into a modern country. The government built factories and new cities. But Stalin was a harsh ruler and sent millions of people to prison camps. Many of them died there of cold or starvation. (*See* **Stalin, Joseph.**)

In World War II, the Soviet Union fought on the same side as Britain and the United States against Nazi Germany. No nation suffered more from the war than the Soviet Union. German armies destroyed many Soviet cities, and more than 20 million Soviet people lost their lives. Finally, the Allies—Britain, the Soviet Union, and the United States—defeated Germany.

Soon after the war, the United States and the Soviet Union became opponents. They had different forms of government, and each wanted the support of the rest of the world. Both countries built huge reserves of nuclear weapons. They competed against each other in several parts of the world, and even in space. But they never went to war directly against each other.

The Soviet Union and the United States are still opponents. At the same time, they have begun to understand each other better. Their leaders talk with each other, especially about controlling nuclear weapons. Even though they disagree, they are seeking ways to keep the world at peace.

soybean

The soybean is a plant that belongs to the legume family. The beans it produces are very high in *protein*—an important body-building nutrient. In some parts of the world and for people who do not eat meat, soybean products are major sources of protein. Soybeans are also fed to farm animals and used to make nonfood products.

In the United States, soybeans are the third-largest crop after corn and wheat. The U.S. soybean crop is also the world's largest. Most of it is sold to other nations. Brazil and China, too, grow large amounts of soybeans.

The soybean plant is an *annual*—it sprouts from a seed and completes its life cycle in one growing season. Small white or purple flowers develop into pods that hold two or three yellow or brownish beans. Like other legumes, soybeans have nitrogen-fixing bacteria living on their roots. These bacteria take nitrogen gas from the air and make nitrogen compounds from it. Proteins are nitrogen compounds, so these bacteria help the plants produce beans rich in protein. (*See* **nitrogen.**)

Soybeans are used in several ways. Some soybeans are cooked and eaten whole, but most undergo some processing. They may be cleaned, crushed, and ground into soy meal. Some soy meal is added to animal feed, and some is made into soy protein concentrate. This high-protein concentrate can be made into foods that look and taste like meat. Other soybean food products include soy milk and bean curd, which is often called *tofu.* Fermented soybean paste, called *miso,* is added to soy sauce.

The oil extracted from soybeans is used for cooking and to make margarine, mayonnaise, and other food products. Soy oil is also used in products we do not eat. It goes into soap, paint, ink, woodstains, plastics, and cosmetics.

The soybean plant was cultivated in China 5,000 years ago. It was brought to Europe in the 1700s and then to the United States. In the early 1900s in the United States, soybeans were raised only for animal feed. After the processes for making meal and extracting oil were improved, the soybean became a more important crop. Today, many people see soybeans as a way to ease the world's food shortage. The amount of protein produced by an acre planted in soybeans is ten times greater than what is produced by beef cattle living on an acre. Experts hope more people will add soybeans to their diets.

A field of soybean plants (below). The bean itself is inside a fuzzy shell (left).

space exploration

Space exploration has helped us to understand more about outer space and the planets in our solar system. Before space exploration began, astronomers could study outer space only from Earth. Since the 1950s, spacecraft have been sent into space to send back photographs and other information. Astronauts, too, have gone into space and come back with reports.

People have dreamed of going to the moon for centuries. As long ago as the year 150, a Greek writer named Lucian wrote about an imaginary trip to the moon. Some stories of trips to the moon were adventure stories. In Jules Verne's famous stories *From the Earth to the Moon* and *Around the Moon,* written in the 1800s, astronauts traveled inside a shell fired from a huge cannon.

Rockets Spacecraft are launched into space by rockets. Unlike airplanes, rockets can fly where there is no atmosphere. Rockets also travel much faster than planes. Rockets need this tremendous speed to escape Earth's gravity and to get high enough to put a satellite or an astronaut into orbit.

Scientists at Johnson Space Center in Houston, Texas, track the astronauts as they speed toward the moon.

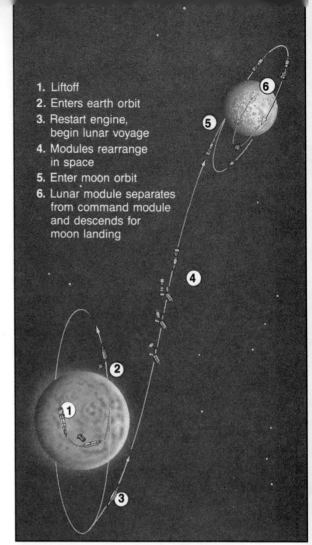

1. Liftoff
2. Enters earth orbit
3. Restart engine, begin lunar voyage
4. Modules rearrange in space
5. Enter moon orbit
6. Lunar module separates from command module and descends for moon landing

Astronauts on their way to the moon first orbit Earth, then fly 250,000 miles, orbit the moon, and finally land.

The first rockets were made about 800 years ago by the Chinese. These rockets were propelled by gunpowder. German scientists designed large guided missiles for use in World War II, during the early 1940s. These speedy V-2 rockets were powered by liquid fuel. After the war, the United States and the Soviet Union used German rocket technology to design even larger rockets. Those rockets were eventually used in early space exploration. (*See* rocket.)

Satellites Space exploration began in 1957 with the launching of *Sputnik,* a Soviet satellite the size of a large beachball. A satellite is an object that travels around a planet in a path called its *orbit. Sputnik* was sent into space by huge rockets developed in the Soviet Union.

Astronauts explored the moon's desertlike surface in a car called a *lunar rover.*
The sky appears black even in sunlight, because the moon has no atmosphere.

The launching of *Sputnik* started the "space race" between the Soviet Union and the United States. During 1957, the Soviet Union put *Sputnik II* into orbit. In January 1958, the United States put its first satellite, *Explorer 1,* into orbit. These satellites added greatly to our knowledge of both Earth and outer space. (*See* **satellite.**)

Human Space Travel In the early years of space exploration, scientists did not know enough about outer space to get a human into space and back alive. Just getting up into space is dangerous. Astronauts ride in a small satellite at the tip of a huge rocket. Many rockets, powered by millions of gallons of explosive fuel, have blown up. Also, the tremendous speed of takeoff creates danger for the astronauts.

Once in space, the astronauts depend entirely on their satellite, called a *space capsule.* People need special equipment and protection to survive in space. The spacecraft and the astronauts' space suits must keep them at the right temperature, and protect them from the sun's radiation. The spacecraft must carry air for the astronauts and be strong enough that stray meteoroids will not puncture it. (*See* **astronaut.**)

A safe return to Earth presents other problems. A space capsule orbits Earth above the atmosphere. On the way down, it reenters the atmosphere. *Friction*—rubbing together —with the atmosphere helps to slow down

the capsule, which is good, but creates a lot of heat, which is bad. To keep space capsules from burning up during reentry, specially designed heat shields are attached to them.

By 1961, scientists were confident that they had solved these problems. On April 12, 1961, the Soviet cosmonaut Yuri Gagarin became the first human to go into space. He completed one orbit of Earth, lasting 1 hour and 48 minutes. Three weeks later, Alan B. Shepard, Jr., became the first American in space. His 15-minute flight took him into space but not into orbit. On February 20, 1962, John Glenn, Jr., became the first American to go into orbit. He circled Earth three times in 4 hours and 55 minutes.

By the late 1960s, the United States was ready for a manned trip to the moon. On July 16, 1969, U.S. astronauts Neil Armstrong, Edwin Aldrin, Jr., and Michael Collins blasted off for the moon. Three days later, their *Apollo* spacecraft went into orbit around the moon. On July 20, Armstrong and Aldrin went down to the moon's surface in the *lunar lander.* Armstrong became the first person to set foot on the moon. He and Aldrin explored near the lunar lander and collected rock samples. They returned to Earth safely on July 24.

The next big goal in space exploration was to establish a permanent—long-lasting— space station where people could live for a long time. As a first step, the United States and the Soviet Union each launched experimental space stations in the 1970s. These experimental stations stayed in orbit and teams of astronauts went up to them and back in rockets. (*See* **space station.**)

By the late 1970s, the U.S. space program focused on developing a *space shuttle.* The shuttle is a rocket-powered spacecraft that can make repeated trips into space and back. The shuttle could be especially useful for building and maintaining a space station. People believe that the Soviet Union is building a similar craft which is being called a *space plane.*

The first space shuttle flew on April 12, 1981. Over the next few years, space shuttles took off frequently. But on January 28, 1986, the tragic explosion of the space shuttle *Challenger* during takeoff killed seven astronauts. Shuttle flights were stopped until rockets with better safety features could be

The space shuttle, shown as it blasts off, can return from orbit and be reused.

Astronauts train for many months to learn to fly the shuttle.

built. The accident reminded everyone that space travel is still very dangerous.

Spaceprobes The U.S. and Soviet space programs also explore space by sending out *spaceprobes.* Spaceprobes are spacecraft sent out to collect scientific information. They carry scientific instruments and can travel to places where people cannot yet go. Spaceprobes have explored the sun, moon, and every planet in the solar system except Pluto at close range. Much of what we know about planets today and all of the close-up pictures of planets come from spaceprobes.

Spaceprobes do not orbit Earth but are launched out into space. Some spaceprobes are programmed to land on a planet, others to orbit it, and still others to fly close by. Once a spaceprobe reaches its goal, the instruments perform experiments and take readings and pictures. This information is radioed to Earth, where scientists study it.

Spaceprobes must also carry such equipment as power-generating systems, control computers, and communications gear. A spaceprobe such as *Voyager 2*—which carried out a mission to the planets Jupiter, Saturn, Uranus, and Neptune—has three

COMET HALLEY   HALLEY MULTICOLOUR CAMERA   13–MAR–1986

IMAGE #3416 – 25 600 km   IMAGE #3444 – 18 000 km   IMAGE #3461 – 13 400 km

IMAGE #3475 – 9 600 km   IMAGE #3491 – 5 200 km   IMAGE #3496 – 3 900 km

Above, Halley's comet as seen in 1986 by *Giotto,* a spaceprobe sent up by the European Space Agency. The pictures show a giant, irregular "snowball" made of minerals and ice crystals. Below, Saturn's rings as seen by the U.S. *Voyager 1.*

small nuclear generators to supply power. Six onboard computers take care of many of the routine functions aboard the spaceprobe. Communications gear sends the information collected by *Voyager* across billions of miles of space to Earth. *Voyager* also has onboard computers to keep it on course and small rockets that can change its course.

Both the United States and Soviet Union began sending out spaceprobes in the years following *Sputnik.* The United States *Viking* spaceprobes studied Mars. The Soviet *Venera* spaceprobes studied Venus. The spaceprobes with the most daring aims have been the U.S. spaceprobes *Voyager 2* and *Viking 1* and *Viking 2.* The two *Viking* spaceprobes landed on Mars in 1975. *Voyager 2* has been traveling toward the outer reaches of the solar system since 1977.

An artist's view of a space station that will orbit Earth. Solar panels at both ends collect energy for the station. Work and living modules are attached to the middle. A space shuttle (upper left) is leaving the station.

space station

A space station is a large spacecraft designed to orbit Earth for years and serve as a base for space exploration. A space station must provide comfortable living and work areas for a crew of astronauts, scientists, and technicians. From a space station, scientists will be able to conduct long-term studies of space that cannot be performed from Earth. They will be able to study Earth in ways not possible before.

A rocket launched from Earth requires a lot of fuel. It must reach a very high speed to pass through the atmosphere and escape Earth's gravity. A rocket launched from a space station does not need the same power, since it starts out beyond Earth's gravity and

atmosphere. Most of its fuel can be used for cruising. A space station can serve as a stopover for astronauts on their way to the moon or Mars. It can also be a base for refueling or repairing broken spacecraft.

The weightlessness in a space station makes it a good place to manufacture certain products. For example, tiny plastic balls used in measurement tools have been made in space. Had they been made here on Earth, gravity would have made them less than perfectly round.

Building a Space Station The United States and the Soviet Union each began planning a permanent space station in the 1960s. Before the idea could become a reality, scientists had to learn more about space. They had to figure out how to construct and

space, the work will be slow and tiring. Working outside a spacecraft is also dangerous for the astronauts.

Experimental Space Stations The Soviet Union and the United States put experimental space stations into orbit in the early 1970s. These stations were small enough to be put into orbit in one piece. Later, astronauts traveled to the space stations aboard a different rocket.

The Soviet space station *Salyut I* went into orbit in 1971. This 25-foot-long station was supposed to stay permanently in orbit, but it fell back to Earth after six months.

The United States launched its experimental station, *Skylab,* in 1973. Between 1973 and 1974, three separate crews lived and worked in the station for weeks at a time. *Skylab* was not planned as a permanent space station. It was abandoned after the third mission and fell to Earth in 1979. Most of it burned away as it reentered Earth's atmosphere, and the rest fell harmlessly in Australia and into the Indian Ocean.

During the 1970s and early 1980s, the Soviets successfully put a number of *Salyut* stations into orbit and set new records for time spent in space. For example, in 1984, a three-man crew aboard *Salyut VII* spent 237 days in space.

The Soviet space station program took another major step forward in 1986, when they launched *Mir. Mir* is intended as a base unit for a larger station. Unlike previous *Salyut* stations, *Mir* is set up entirely as living quarters. It has a dining area for six crew members and about as much room as a medium-size house trailer. At one end, there are five docking ports, where new sections can be added. These new sections could contain scientific labs.

The United States plans to put a full-size, permanent space station into operation during the 1990s. The station will start out with a crew of six to eight people. Fresh crews and supplies will be brought up from Earth every three months aboard a space shuttle.

See also **space exploration.**

equip the space station so it would operate reliably. A full-size station would be too large to send up in one rocket. Scientists needed to know how to send all the parts for the space station and have them all meet where they could be put together.

Designing a station to operate for long periods in space is a complicated problem. There must be a source of electric power to run all of the space station's equipment. There must be equipment to produce air for the crew members to breathe. There must be equipment to keep living areas and work areas at a comfortable temperature.

The machinery needed to do this must be assembled in space, a section at a time. Astronauts wearing bulky space suits must work outside their spacecraft to position the sections and make electrical connections. Even though everything is weightless in

Spain

Capital: Madrid
Area: 194,896 square miles (504,781 square kilometers)
Population (1985): about 38,829,000
Official language: Castilian Spanish

Spain is a large country in southwestern Europe. It covers most of the Iberian Peninsula, between the Atlantic Ocean and the Mediterranean Sea. Spain once had a wealthy and powerful empire, with lands in North and South America, Africa, and the Pacific Islands. Today, Spain is known for its beauty and rich history.

Land To the east and south, Spain borders the Mediterranean Sea. Africa is less than 10 miles (16 kilometers) away, across the Strait of Gibraltar. In the north, Spain borders France and the Atlantic. Part of its western edge touches the Atlantic, and the rest borders Portugal.

Most of Spain is a high, dry plateau called the Meseta. Mountains and rolling hills rise from the Meseta. Some of the mountains are higher than 11,000 feet (3,300 meters) above sea level. In the hills, herders raise sheep and goats. Despite dry weather and poor soil, much of the Meseta is used for farming. The main crops are wheat, olives, wine grapes, and citrus fruits.

The best farming regions are near the Ebro River, in the northeast, and the Guadalquivir River, in the southwest. Little rain falls in these regions, but irrigation systems bring water to the fields.

In the northeast, the rugged Pyrenees Mountains separate Spain from France. They are covered with forests and with grazing land for cattle. Other mountain ranges continue along northern Spain to the Atlantic. Caves in these mountains contain some of the world's oldest paintings.

People About three-fourths of all Spaniards live in towns or cities. Madrid, the capital and largest city in Spain, is near the center of the country. The busy port city of Barcelona is in the northeast corner, on the Mediterranean. Madrid, Barcelona, and Bilbao, a port city on the Atlantic, are also centers of manufacturing. Spain's factories produce cars, ships, leather goods, and steel and chemical products.

Most Spanish city dwellers live in apartment houses, and work in stores, offices, or factories. In Spanish cities, many businesses close during the hottest part of the day. Workers go home to rest for a few hours. They return around four o'clock and work later in the evening.

The Basque (BAHSK) people live in villages in the Pyrenees of Spain and France. They have their own traditions and language. They are skilled at fishing and herding. The Basques are also known for their dances.

History People have been living in Spain for 100,000 years. About 5,000 years ago, people called Iberians were settling villages in Spain. They lived by farming and fishing. Around 1000 B.C., Phoenician traders set up colonies in southern and eastern Spain. They were followed by settlers from Greece and Africa.

About 200 B.C., the Romans took control of Spain. They built roads, towns, and *aqueducts*—raised stone channels for water. Their language, Latin, became the basis of the Spanish language. (*See* **Spanish.**)

After the year 700, Moors from northern Africa entered Spain. They brought the Islamic religion and knowledge of medicine, astronomy, and mathematics. They built beautiful mosques, palaces, and gardens that you can still visit. The Moors ruled until the 1000s, when Christians defeated them.

Beginning in the late 1400s, several European nations began sending expeditions to find a sea route to Asia. The king and queen of Spain, Ferdinand and Isabella, sent Christopher Columbus west across the Atlantic.

Bay of Biscay

La Coruña • Gijón • Santander • San Sebastián

Oviedo • Bilbao • Pamplona

FRANCE

ANDORRA

P Y R E N E E S

Vigo •

Ebro River

Valladolid • Duero River • Saragossa

Barcelona •

SPAIN

★ Madrid

BALEARIC ISLANDS

Minorca

Tagus River • Toledo •

Valencia •

Palma • Majorca

ELEVATION Feet

Guadiana River

Ibiza

Over 10000
5000- 10000
2000- 5000
1000- 2000
0- 1000

Alicante •

100

Murcia •

Miles

Cordoba • River

Cartagena •

Mediterranean Sea

Seville • Guadalquivir

Granada •

ATLANTIC OCEAN

SIERRA NEVADA

Jerez •

Malaga •

Cadiz •

Marbella •

Gibraltar
(Br.)

Strait of
Gibraltar

**A town in Andalusia,
a region in southern Spain.**

He claimed Cuba for Spain. Soon, other Spanish explorers claimed much of Central and South America, and parts of North America. They brought their language and religion to these regions. They returned to Spain with gold and silver.

For the next 200 years, Spain enjoyed a golden age in painting, music, dance, and literature. Novels written by Cervantes in the 1600s are still read. Paintings from this time hang in many of the world's museums.

In 1898, the United States went to war with Spain, partly over Cuban independence. Spain lost the last of its colonies in the Americas. (*See* **Spanish-American War.**)

Kings and queens ruled Spain until 1931, when Spain became a republic. But groups within the Spanish Republic fought for control. In 1936, this conflict became the Spanish Civil War. In 1939, the side led by General Francisco Franco won. Franco ruled as dictator until he died, in 1975. Since then, Spain has become more democratic.

43

Spanish

Spanish is the language of Spain, Mexico, and most countries of Central America and South America. Spanish developed from Latin, the language of the ancient Romans. For this reason, it is called a *Romance language.* Other Romance languages include French, Italian, and Portuguese.

Nearly 300 million people learn Spanish as their *first language*—the language spoken at home. Only three other languages are learned by more people as a first language. These are Mandarin Chinese, Hindi—one of the languages of India—and English.

Spanish is widely spoken in Florida and the southwestern part of the United States. Many words in the English language, such as *vanilla, rodeo,* and *alligator,* came from Spanish.

In the 200s B.C., the ancient Romans invaded the Iberian Peninsula—where the countries of Spain and Portugal are today. The people in Iberia slowly began adding the Latin of the Romans to their own language. Over the years, their language changed into a new language—Spanish. People throughout Iberia speak *dialects*—slightly different forms—of Spanish. When the Spanish province of Castile became a leading center of government, more people began using the Castilian dialect. Today, millions of people in Spain and other countries speak Castilian Spanish. Another dialect developed into the Portuguese language.

Spanish explorers and settlers in the Americas added American Indian words to their language. This form of Spanish is called American Spanish. American Spanish and Castilian Spanish are very similar. But there are differences in the sounds and meanings of some words.

The Spanish and English alphabets are much the same. But the letter *w* is not part of the Spanish alphabet. Spanish also has four letters that are not included in the English alphabet. These are *ch, ll, ñ,* and *rr.* Even though three of these are written with

SOME EVERYDAY SPANISH PHRASES	
buenos dias	good morning
hasta luego	goodbye
por favor	please
gracias	thank you
¿Cómó está usted?	How are you?
muy bien	very well
¿Como se llame usted?	What is your name?
Me llamo _____ .	My name is _____ .

two letters, they are considered one letter in Spanish. The letters *ch* and *ll* have their own sections in the Spanish dictionary. The letter *rr* does not, because it is never used to begin a word.

Spanish is a *phonetic* language. This means that each letter stands for one sound, and words are pronounced the way they are written. Some sounds in Spanish are different from English sounds, and many English sounds are not heard in Spanish.

Spanish-American War

The Spanish-American War was a conflict in which the United States helped Cuba win independence from Spain. The war lasted from April to December 1898. It made the United States a world power.

Cuba is a small island about 90 miles (144 kilometers) south of the United States. It had been ruled by Spain since the late 1400s. During the 1800s, the Cubans began to rebel against Spain. In 1895, Spain sent troops to crush a Cuban rebellion, and thousands of Cubans were killed. When U.S. newspapers reported the event, many Americans sided with the Cubans.

In early 1898, riots broke out in Cuba's capital city, Havana. To protect American citizens and property there, the United States sent the battleship *Maine* into Havana's harbor. On the night of February 15, an explosion ripped through the *Maine,* killing 266 of its crew.

No one ever learned what caused the explosion, but U.S. newspapers claimed that the Spanish blew up the ship. An angry cry went up—"Remember the *Maine!*" People wanted the U.S. government to attack the Spanish in Cuba. On April 25, the United States declared war on Spain.

The fighting began in the Spanish-controlled Philippine Islands. At daybreak on April 30, U.S. ships attacked the Spanish fleet in the harbor of Manila, the Philippine capital. They destroyed all the Spanish ships and lost none of their own.

In June, U.S. troops landed in Cuba. Among them was a cavalry regiment called the "Rough Riders." Theodore Roosevelt, who organized the regiment, later became president of the United States. On July 1, the U.S. troops defeated the Spanish armed forces on San Juan Hill and Kettle Hill. (*See* **Roosevelt, Theodore.**)

American troops defeat the Spanish in Cuba. Spain's ships are trapped by the U.S. Navy.

Meanwhile, at the Cuban port city of Santiago, U.S. ships had trapped another Spanish fleet. On July 3, the Spanish ships tried to escape, but all were destroyed. On July 17, the Spanish commander at Santiago surrendered. On August 13, the Spanish troops fighting in the Philippines surrendered.

Spain and the United States signed a peace treaty in Paris on December 10, 1898. Spain granted Cuba independence. It also gave the islands of Puerto Rico and Guam to the United States, and sold the Philippines to the United States for $20 million.

See also **Cuba.**

speaking

Speaking is the act of saying words and sentences. People speak to communicate with each other and to exchange ideas. Actors, television and radio announcers, teachers, religious leaders, and politicians all have jobs that depend partly on speaking clearly and well. Since most of us use spoken language to communicate, we need good speaking skills. Good speakers choose their words carefully, pronounce them clearly, organize their ideas, and pay attention to how their listeners are responding.

Most humans are born with the ability to make sounds. Babies learn to speak by listening to and imitating the sounds people make.

You don't think about the complicated physical process of speaking very often. When you speak, you breathe out. The flow of air passes between the vocal cords in your throat and makes them *vibrate*—move rapidly back and forth. The vibrations create the sound. The sound of your voice is also affected by the shapes of your nasal passages and mouth, and how you move your lips, tongue, and jaw.

Speech *rhythm*—the way sounds flow within words and between words—can be a source of trouble for some people. They may *stutter*—repeat a sound at the beginning of a word. They may *stammer*—stop between words. *Speech therapists*—people with special training—are often able to help others overcome these problems. Doctors and dentists can sometimes correct speech difficulties caused by mouth problems.

People used to think that deaf people also could not speak. Actually, most deaf people have the ability to speak. But if they have never heard sounds, it is difficult for them to learn how. Special training has helped many deaf people to speak. Even if they cannot hear, they can learn to imitate sounds by watching a screen that shows sound waves. They can see the shape of the waves made by the proper sound and then try to match it

This gifted speaker informs and entertains her audience. They listen eagerly.

with their own sound. Teachers help deaf people learn how to place their teeth and tongues and how to shape their lips to pronounce words. People with some hearing may use powerful headphones to hear sounds.

See also **language** and **sign language.**

speed

Speed is the measure of how fast something moves. We measure speed by describing how far something travels in a certain amount of time. For example, car speeds are measured in miles per hour or kilometers per hour.

HOW FAST CAN THEY GO?

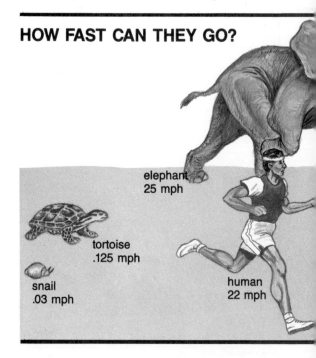

elephant
25 mph

tortoise
.125 mph

snail
.03 mph

human
22 mph

A *speedometer* is a measuring device that tells how fast a car is going. If a car travels at a steady speed of 30 miles per hour, it will travel half a mile each minute, and 30 miles in 60 minutes—one hour. But cars and other vehicles usually do not travel at a steady speed. They *accelerate*—gain speed—when the driver presses harder on the gas pedal. They *decelerate*—slow down—when the driver presses less hard on the gas pedal. Still, the average speed of the car can be figured out by dividing the distance covered by the amount of time it took to cover it.

A spaceship may travel 24,000 miles per hour. It may be easier to understand how fast that is if you think of this speed as 600 miles per minute, or 10 miles per second.

If we are measuring the speed of something traveling very slowly, we need to use still other units of speed. For example, it is difficult to measure a snail's speed in miles per hour. It may travel only 5 feet in a day. So we probably would measure the snail's speed in inches or centimeters per hour.

One special measure of speed is the *mach* —the speed of sound in air. At first, jet aircraft could not go faster than Mach 1—about 600 miles per hour (960 kilometers per hour). The aircraft would begin to shake so much it might break apart. Today, some specially designed aircraft, such as the Concorde, can go faster than Mach 1. The Concorde's top speed is a little over Mach 2—twice the speed of sound. The speed of jet fighter planes is measured in mach numbers.

What is the fastest speed of all? Nothing in the universe can travel faster than the speed of light—exactly 299,792,458 meters per second. This is about 300,000 kilometers or 186,000 miles per second. Light from the sun travels 149 million kilometers (93 million miles) to Earth in just a little more than 8 minutes.

spice

A spice is a flavoring that comes from a plant. Spices usually have a pleasantly strong, sweet smell and an interesting taste. Some well-known spices are pepper, mustard, cinnamon, ginger, nutmeg, and cloves. Herbs, too, are used to season foods, and they are sometimes grouped with spices.

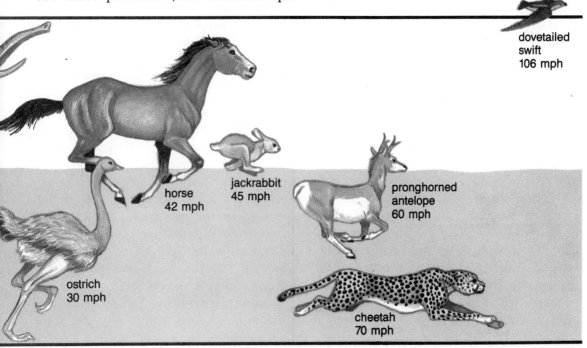

dovetailed
swift
106 mph

horse
42 mph

jackrabbit
45 mph

pronghorned
antelope
60 mph

ostrich
30 mph

cheetah
70 mph

thyme leaves

sage leaves

cinnamon bark

clove flower buds

nutmeg seeds

paprika fruit

mustard seeds

mint leaves

pepper berries

lemon balm leaves

ginger root

Spices add flavor to foods. They may come from any part of a plant—
the root, seed, berry, leaf, bud, or flower.

But spices grow in tropical regions, and most herbs grow in temperate climates. (*See* **herb.**)

Spices come from different parts of various plants. After harvesting, the plant parts are often dried, ground, or powdered to make them easy to add to foods. Black pepper and white pepper are from the fruit of an East Indian pepper plant. Cinnamon comes from tree bark. Ginger is the root of the ginger plant. Nutmeg is the seed of a tropical tree. Cloves are the buds of still another kind of tree. Several spices may be blended to produce a special taste. The spice we sometimes call *curry,* used in Indian cooking, is a mixture of spices and herbs.

When we think of the cooking of a region or nation, we often think of certain flavors. Those flavors usually come from the spices used. Chinese cooking often uses ginger, pepper, and anise. Indian cooking uses spices such as cumin, coriander, turmeric, and chili.

In ancient times, merchants from Arabia and southern Europe traveled thousands of miles to China and Java for spices. The spices could be sold for a high price in Greece, Rome, and Egypt. People needed spices to help keep food from spoiling and to cover up the bad taste of foods that were beginning to spoil.

After the fall of ancient Rome—around the year 500—few spices were available in Europe. In the 1200s, Marco Polo and other Europeans traveled to Asia and came back with reports of spices. The spice trade began again and brought wealth to Venice and Genoa, two cities in Italy. The desire for spices drove European explorers to search for a sea route around the tip of Africa. Columbus sailed westward to reach India and southeast Asia, where spices grew. Spices were among the reasons leading to Magellan's voyage around the world. Magellan wanted to find the Spice Islands—the Moluccas—and settle the question of whether they belonged to Spain or Portugal. Later, Portugal, the Netherlands, and Britain set up colonies in Asia. They wanted to control the production and trade of spices.

spider

Spiders are animals well known for spinning silken webs. Spiders are sometimes confused with insects, but they are not insects. They actually belong to a class of animals called *arachnids.* Ticks, scorpions, and daddy longlegs are some other kinds of arachnids. Insects have antennae, and spiders do not. Insects have both compound eyes and simple eyes. Spiders have only simple eyes. Most insects have wings, but spiders do not. Insects have six legs, while spiders have eight.

There are more than 25,000 kinds of spiders. They are found throughout the world in all kinds of environments. They live along seashores, on mountaintops, in deserts, swamps, caves, houses, fields, and forests. Spiders are important in the food chain. They eat many insects and are food for birds, frogs, lizards, and snakes.

Insects are the main food of spiders. Most spiders have poison glands connected to sharp fangs near the mouth. As soon as a spider grabs a victim, it injects poison to paralyze and kill it. When the spider is ready to eat its meal, it injects the insect with digestive juices. These break down the soft parts of the insect, forming a soupy liquid. The spider then sucks up the liquid.

Spiders' Silk In the spider's *abdomen* —the last section of its body—there are silk glands that make liquid silk. Some of the glands produce silk that stays sticky. The liquid passes to the *spinnerets*—the spinning organs. The spinnerets can produce a thin thread or a thick one. As the liquid silk passes from the spinnerets, it hardens into silk thread.

The silk has many uses. Spiders build their webs with silk, line their nests with it, and wrap their victims in it. Female spiders spin silk cases around their eggs to protect them. Wherever a spider goes, it leaves behind a line of silk called a *dragline.* If danger threatens, the spider can drop down to safety on its dragline.

Three kinds of webs built to catch food— orb, funnel, and sheet webs.

Spiders, especially young ones, may be carried a long way on their silk. A spider climbs to the top of a plant. When the wind blows, the spider spins out long silk threads. The wind lifts the threads and the spider floats off.

Kinds of Spiders Each kind of web-spinning spider makes its own kind of web. Some spin large, flat sheets. Others spin webs shaped like funnels or like delicate wheels. The webs have both sticky threads and dry ones. The sticky threads are for trapping insects. The spider can run freely over the dry threads.

A web-spinning spider usually waits in the center of its web for meals. As soon as an insect gets caught in the web, the spider rushes over, injects it with poison, and wraps it for eating later.

A few kinds of spiders do not spin webs. The *trap-door spider* lives in a silk-lined burrow covered by a hinged trapdoor. It holds the door slightly open and watches for prey. When a victim comes by, the spider pounces and then pulls the animal into the burrow.

Crab spiders also lie in wait, usually deep in a flower. When an insect crawls into the flower, the crab spider grabs it. Often, the crab spider attacks insects bigger than itself.

Wolf spiders stalk and chase their prey. They usually hunt at night, when the insects they like to eat are active—and their worst enemies, wasps, are resting.

Only one kind of spider is not a land animal. The *water spider* lives underwater. Like other spiders, the water spider breathes air. It forms air bubbles at the surface of the water, carries them down to the bottom of the pond, and stores them in a sac. The water spider uses the sac as a nest—it lays its eggs and raises its young in the sac. When it has used up all the air, the water spider returns to the surface for more.

A few spiders are dangerous to people. The most dangerous spider in the United States is the *black widow.* It is a small black spider with a red mark in the shape of an hourglass on the underside of its abdomen. Black widow spiders live in hidden places, such as under houses or in piles of stones or lumber. Their bite can cause serious harm, especially to young children and the elderly.

Another dangerous spider found in the United States is the *brown recluse.* This dull-colored spider has a faint mark in the shape of a violin on its back. The brown recluse is a shy creature. It lives beneath stones and in other hidden places. Its poison is not powerful enough to kill a person, but it can cause a nasty wound.

Tarantulas are large, furry spiders with long, thick legs. Most kinds live in tropical forests, but some kinds live in the southwestern United States. The largest—found in South America—may have a legspan of 25 centimeters (10 inches). The largest U.S. kinds have a legspan of about 13 centimeters (5 inches). Although the ones found in the United States look frightening, they are seldom dangerous to people.

spinal cord

The spinal cord is a nerve cable that runs through your spine and attaches to the base of the brain. Pairs of *spinal nerves* lead away from the spinal cord. Messages from the brain travel down the spinal cord, through the spinal nerves, and through nerves in the rest of the body. Messages from the various parts of the body travel the opposite way to the brain.

If someone tickles the bottom of your foot, nerves in your foot will send a message to

These spiders are drawn life-size. The tarantula is large and hairy. The black widow and brown recluse have poisonous bites.

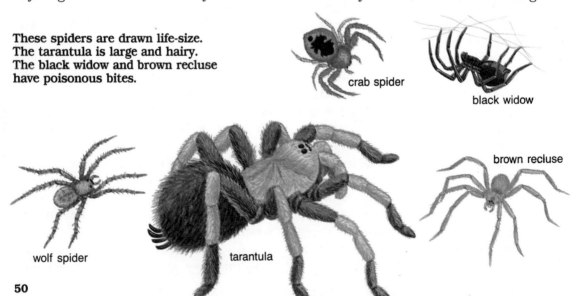

crab spider

black widow

brown recluse

wolf spider

tarantula

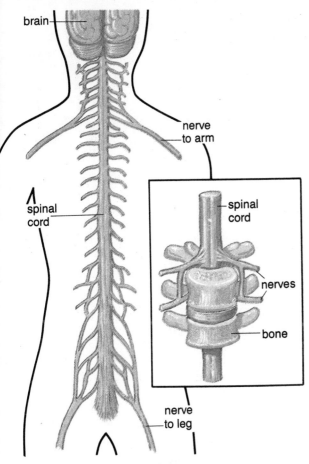

brain

nerve to arm

spinal cord

spinal cord

nerves

bone

nerve to leg

The spinal cord is a nerve cable that runs through the bones of the spine. Smaller nerves branch to many parts of the body.

your spinal cord. The spinal cord sends a message back, telling your muscles to pull your foot away at once.

The spinal cord also sends a message to the brain. Then you become aware of the tickling. You make decisions about what other things to do. Messages from the brain travel down the spinal cord and out to your muscles. Your muscles move as they have been directed—pushing the tickler away or trying to tickle back.

The spinal cord cannot repair itself. If it is cut, there is permanent paralysis of the body from that place downward. No messages can travel to or from that part of the body.

See also **nerve** and **skeleton.**

sponge

The sponge is an unusual animal that lives in water. It has no head, mouth, arms, legs,

heart, or stomach. Its body is hollow. Many small openings, called *pores,* lead from its hollow center to the outside. Water enters some of the pores and leaves through other pores. As the water passes through, the sponge captures the oxygen and bits of food in it.

The soft body of a sponge is supported by a skeleton. The skeletons of some sponges are made of tiny needles. Other sponges have skeletons made of tough fibers. Still others have both needles and fibers.

There are about 5,000 kinds of sponges. The smallest are only 1 millimeter (1/2 inch) wide. The largest may be 1.8 meters (6 feet) across. Sponges take many forms. Some even branch like trees.

Sponges live in all the oceans. A few kinds of sponges live in fresh water. No sponges live on land.

People gather some sponges with soft fiber skeletons. The sponges are killed and dried. The skeletons are then cleaned and sold. These sponges soak up a lot of water. They are used for bathing and for washing cars and floors. But today, most "sponges" are imitations made of rubber or plastic.

The sponge is an animal that spends its entire life underwater.

Sports are played by teams or by individuals. Achievement may be measured in points, scores, or time. Many people play sports for fun and relaxation.

sports

Sports are games, exercises, or activities that people take part in for fun, fitness, or both. Sports are a great way to get physical exercise, something everyone needs in order to stay healthy.

Not all sports are team sports, and not all sports involve winning or losing. Hiking, skiing, swimming, and bicycling are sports that you can enjoy as an individual without having to "win." Other sports, such as tennis and racquetball, are games people play against one another. Popular team sports include baseball, basketball, football, volleyball, hockey, and soccer. Team members must learn to play well together. Team sports test both your athletic ability and your ability to work and cooperate with others.

Athletes may compete in sports on either an *amateur* or a *professional* basis. Professionals are paid to play. Amateurs must not accept payment, or they can no longer compete as amateurs.

For many people, the best place to get started in sports is at school. Almost all elementary and junior high schools in the United States have sports programs for boys and girls. In addition, about 20,000 U.S. high schools offer sports programs. Every year, more than 5 million young athletes compete in school sports. The most talented sometimes go on to play sports in college, and later on as professionals.

Sports clubs or leagues are other good places to get started in a sport. Young baseball players can join Little League teams. Track athletes and gymnasts often join clubs that practice together and take part in competitions. School and league coaches teach the skills needed for playing a sport. They also keep a team organized and working together.

Only the very best athletes are asked to compete in professional team sports, such as baseball, football, basketball, and hockey. Some individual sports—such as tennis, golf, and bowling—are also played on a professional level. Professional sports are a big business in the United States. More than 60 million Americans pay to attend sports events each year. Millions more watch on television. A top professional athlete can earn more than $1 million a year.

Many young athletes dream of being professional stars. Becoming a star athlete takes talent, years of practice, and luck. For most people, simply playing a sport is rewarding in itself.

See the Index for entries on individual sports.

spring, *see* season

spring

A spring is a flow of water from under the ground. Most springwater is cold and good to drink. Some springs are hot, and the water may have bad-tasting minerals dissolved in it. But many people believe these mineral waters have healing powers.

Water from rain and melting snow trickles down into the ground until it reaches the *water table.* The water table is a layer of ground so full of water that it cannot hold any more. (*See* **water table.**)

Where the water table reaches the surface, water will flow from the soil or rock. This flow is a spring. Small springs may flow only part of the year. They may slow down or stop altogether during hot, dry weather. But a large spring will flow all year long. The water flowing from a large spring can feed a stream, which may grow from other springs along its banks.

Steam rises from hot springs in New Zealand.

Hot springs occur in places where the water table is heated by hot, volcanic rocks that are deep down in the ground. In some places—such as Yellowstone National Park in the northwestern United States—the water table is so close to these hot rocks that the water boils and turns to steam. Then, when it comes rushing out of the ground, the steam and boiling water shoot up into the air as a geyser. (*See* **geyser.**)

spy

A spy is a person who mingles with the enemy to learn their secrets. A spy may even work with the enemy, pretending to be one of them. Spies are especially useful in wartime, to find out about enemy plans. Spies captured during wartime are usually put to death.

Spies have many ways of gathering information. Some spies may make friends with the enemy. Others secretly watch people, military installations, troop movements, and so on. They may read people's mail or place tiny electronic devices called "bugs" in people's homes or offices so that they can listen in on telephone conversations.

Modern technology has provided new spying methods. Spy planes and satellites equipped with powerful cameras can take pictures of objects thousands of feet below. In the 1960s, such pictures revealed that the Soviet Union was building missile-launching sites in nearby Cuba. President John F. Kennedy issued a warning to the Soviets, who removed the missile sites.

One of the most famous American spies was Nathan Hale. During the Revolutionary War, he spied on the British forces on Long Island. The British caught him, and he was hanged the very next day. It is thought that his last words were, "I only regret that I have but one life to lose for my country."

See also **codes and ciphers.**

squid, *see* octopuses and squid

The gray squirrel and the southern flying squirrel are both tree squirrels.

squirrels and chipmunks

Squirrels and chipmunks are mammals related to mice and other rodents. Like all rodents, they have two pairs of large front teeth for gnawing. They eat nuts, buds, stems, and roots. (*See* **rodent**.)

These animals live in most parts of the world and are common in North America. There are three main kinds of squirrels—*tree squirrels, flying squirrels,* and *ground squirrels*. Chipmunks are a kind of ground squirrel.

Tree squirrels are often seen in the daytime in gardens, woods, and city parks. They build their nests high in trees and come down to the ground to look for food. Some, such as the gray squirrel, are easily tamed and will accept food from people. Whenever food is plentiful, the squirrels store large amounts in various hiding places. Later, they use their excellent sense of smell to find the hidden food.

The ground squirrel (left) and the chipmunk (right) have similar coloring.

chipmunk

ground squirrel

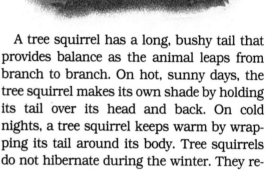

A tree squirrel has a long, bushy tail that provides balance as the animal leaps from branch to branch. On hot, sunny days, the tree squirrel makes its own shade by holding its tail over its head and back. On cold nights, a tree squirrel keeps warm by wrapping its tail around its body. Tree squirrels do not hibernate during the winter. They remain active all year.

Flying squirrels do not have wings, and they cannot fly. They have a fold of skin on each side between the front and back legs. When a flying squirrel stretches out its legs, this loose skin stretches out, too. The flying squirrel can then glide gently down to a lower branch. When it lands, it quickly runs around to the other side of the tree—in case an owl or other enemy followed it. Flying squirrels are active at night. During the day, they sleep in their dens in tree holes. They do not hibernate.

Chipmunks live in underground burrows. One of the best known is the *eastern chipmunk*. It has red-brown fur with black and white stripes across its face and along the sides of its back. It is active during the day and can be easily tamed. A tame chipmunk will take food from your hand. It may not eat the food right away. Instead, it may store the food in large pouches in its cheeks and go to its burrow to eat. It stores leftovers for another day. Chipmunks sleep during the winter, but wake up from time to time to eat some of their stored food.

Sri Lanka, *see* Asia

stained glass

Stained glass is colored glass. The colors are not painted on later—they are added as the glass is being made. Pieces of stained glass are then put together to make designs and pictures. When light shines through the glass, the colors glow. Stained glass is used mainly for making windows, especially in churches. It is also used for lampshades, jewelry boxes, and other decorative objects.

A stained-glass object must be carefully planned. The first step is to make a sketch of the design. Next, a paper pattern of each piece in the design is cut out. The pattern pieces are exactly the same size and shape as the glass pieces, and show their colors. The third step is to place each pattern piece on glass of the proper color and cut around it with a glass cutter.

After all the glass pieces are cut, details of the picture, such as faces, are painted onto them. The painted pieces are then baked in a very hot oven. The heat melts the paint and binds it to the glass.

Next, the glass pieces are joined together. This is done by fitting grooved strips of lead around each piece and joining the strips with *solder.* Solder is a metal that, when heated and then cooled, can hold pieces of metal together.

A very large stained-glass object, such as a big window, is made in sections. The sections are held together by metal rods or wires. The entire window is fitted into a wood or metal frame. This frame then goes into the window frame of the building.

The art of making stained glass developed in Europe during the Middle Ages. Until then, large buildings needed strong, thick walls to hold them up. They could not have big windows, because that would have made the walls weak. Starting around the middle of the 1100s, large churches were built in a new way. The walls were supported by pillars and other structures. This meant that the walls could be thinner and that they could have many large windows. Windows of

Part of a stained glass panel made by the Tiffany Studios in 1905.

stained glass became an important part of a church's design. The windows let in light. They also showed stories from the Bible and figures of the saints. A famous cathedral of the Middle Ages, Chartres Cathedral in France, has over 100 large stained-glass windows. (*See* **cathedral.**)

People became interested in stained glass again in the late 1800s. In England, people made beautiful decorative windows. In the early 1900s, artists in the United States developed new techniques and new uses for stained glass. Among the leaders of this movement were John La Farge and Louis Comfort Tiffany. Tiffany became famous for his beautiful stained-glass lampshades and church windows. Several well-known artists, including Georges Rouault and Marc Chagall, have designed stained-glass windows for modern buildings.

See also **glass.**

stalactites and stalagmites

A stalactite (stuh-LACK-tite) is a rock shaped like an icicle that hangs from the ceiling of a cave. It is formed by dripping water that contains the mineral *calcite.* Limestone, marble, and chalk all contain calcite. Small amounts of calcite collect where the water drips from the ceiling. Over many years, the calcite builds up to form a stalactite. As the water keeps dripping, the stalactite grows longer.

Stalagmites (stuh-LAG-mites) form when drops of water land on the floor. Calcite in the water slowly builds up on the floor, forming an upside-down icicle. As the water keeps dripping, the stalagmite grows taller.

Sometimes, drops of water from the tip of a stalactite cause a stalagmite to form right underneath. If the two keep growing, their tips will eventually meet. When a stalactite and a stalagmite grow together, they form a shape called a *column* or *pillar.*

See also cave.

Stalactites and stalagmites in King's Palace, a chamber in Carlsbad Caverns.

Joseph Stalin ruled the Soviet Union from 1929 until 1953.

Stalin, Joseph

Joseph Stalin ruled the Soviet Union for over 20 years. Under his leadership, the nation made great progress in industry and became a world power. But the cost was great, for Joseph Stalin was one of the cruelest rulers in history.

Stalin was born Iosif Vissarionovich Dzhugashvili in 1879. He changed his name to Stalin, which means "man of steel," when he was in his thirties.

Stalin studied to be a priest, but then joined the struggle to overthrow the czar, Russia's emperor. When the Communists took control of Russia in 1917, Stalin became part of the new government. He became *dictator*—absolute ruler—of the Soviet Union in 1929. (*See* **Russian Revolution.**)

Stalin wanted to make his country strong, and he wanted complete control. He thought that Soviet farms and factories would be more productive if the government owned them. People who refused to let the government take over their property were executed or sent to labor camps.

Under Stalin, the Soviet Union helped defeat Germany in World War II. Afterward, he used Soviet power to gain control of several nations in Eastern Europe. He also supported communist North Korean forces during the Korean War. He died in 1953, shortly before the end of the Korean War. (*See* **World War II** and **Korean War.**)

stamp

A postage stamp shows that a government tax has been paid for sending a letter or package. The first stamps were made by pressing—"stamping"—a design into melted wax. That is why they were called stamps.

The very first paper postage stamps were issued by Great Britain in 1840. Within 20 years, most countries of the world were using paper stamps. The first U.S. stamps were printed in 1847. Today, more than 150 countries print postage stamps. The United States prints more stamps than any other country—billions of stamps each year. (*See* **postal service.**)

Stamp collecting is one of the world's most popular hobbies. It is an easy hobby to start, and it does not have to cost a lot of money. Stamps can be beautiful and interesting. People may collect the stamps of just one country or the stamps of many different countries. Through stamp collecting, you can learn about the countries of the world.

To keep your stamp collection, you need a stamp album. It may be a book with pictures of stamps printed on the pages. It can also be a book with blank pages.

If you select an album with blank pages, you must decide how to organize your collection. The most common way to organize a collection is by countries. You might also decide to organize your stamps by the year they were issued, or by the pictures printed on them. For example, you might group stamps with pictures of birds in one part of your album. Those with pictures of famous people might be in another section.

To learn more about stamp collecting, you may join a stamp club. Clubs are great places to trade stamps and information with other collectors. There are also many magazines and books about stamp collecting.

Stamp collections and even single stamps can become very valuable. For example, stamps with printing errors sometimes sell for very high prices. In one of the most famous cases, the picture of an airplane on a 1918 U.S. stamp was printed upside down. Only a few stamps were printed before the mistake was caught. The few that remain are now worth $60,000 each!

You'll enjoy collecting stamps just for the fun of it. If your collection becomes valuable, then that is an added benefit.

See also **collecting.**

Many stamps are rare and valuable. The one at right is the first stamp issued by the United States.

THE LIFE OF A SUN-LIKE STAR

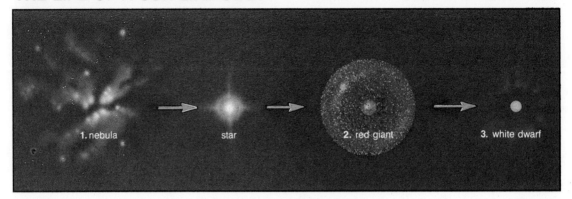

1. The star emerges from a nebula and shines for billions of years.
2. It grows into a red giant. 3. It "burns out," becoming a white dwarf star.

star

A star is a fiery ball of gases that glows by its own energy. Our sun is a star. Our moon and the planets appear to shine, but they are not stars. They only reflect the light from the sun.

To us, stars seem to twinkle. That is because the layers of air in our atmosphere are never entirely still, and the steady light from stars is filtered through them.

When you look up at the sky on a clear night, you can see about 2,000 stars without the aid of a telescope. But there are many more stars than that. Astronomers using the most powerful telescopes can see over 1 billion of them. Astronomers estimate that our galaxy alone—the Milky Way—has at least 100 billion stars. But the Milky Way is only one of many galaxies in the universe, each having billions of stars. (See **Milky Way** and **galaxy**.)

Why can we see only 2,000 stars in our night sky? One reason is that most stars are too far away to see with the naked eye. The sun is easy enough to see because it is the closest star and only about 150 million kilometers (93 million miles) away.

The other stars are much farther away. The next-closest star is Alpha Centauri. It is about 40 trillion kilometers (25 trillion miles) away from Earth. Another way to measure this distance is in light-years. A light-year is the distance light travels in one year. The light from Alpha Centauri takes

more than four years to reach us, so Alpha Centauri is four light-years away. The entire Andromeda Galaxy is more than 2 million light-years away. After traveling all that distance, the light from its 400 billion stars appears in our sky as just a small oval patch. (See **light-year.**)

A Closer Look at the Stars Our sun is the only star close enough for astronomers to study in detail. But astronomers have learned a lot about other stars by studying them with telescopes and other instruments.

The huge mass of a star pushes elements together with such force that the nuclei of their atoms combine to form other elements. This process, called *nuclear fusion,* releases so much energy that the gases in the star glow from the heat.

Stars come in various sizes, but there seem to be limits as to how large or small they can be. A star that has over 150 times the mass of our sun is likely to explode from the pressure inside it. The largest known star is R136a in a nearby galaxy called the Large Cloud of Magellan. This star may have 400 times the mass of our sun. Astronomers also think there are no stars with less than 1/2 of our sun's mass. Objects that small do not begin to burn like a star. Instead, they become planets or other cold, dark objects.

Astronomers have also found that stars often occur in pairs or in groups. Over half of the stars they can see have one or more companion stars. Stars and their companions revolve around each other. A pair of stars are

THE LIFE OF A MASSIVE STAR

nebula   **1.** massive star   **2.** super red giant   **3.** supernova   **4.** neutron star   black hole

1. The star begins much larger than other stars. **2.** It becomes a super red giant.
3. It explodes, becoming a supernova. **4.** It collapses, becoming a dense neutron star.

called *binary stars*. A group of three is called a *triple star*. Alpha Centauri is really a triple star.

Some stars change brightness in regular cycles, brightening and fading over and over. Astronomers know of about 25,000 of these *variable stars*. Their cycles vary, taking anywhere from hours to years to complete.

There are different types of variable stars. In one type, a faint companion star regularly passes in front of a brighter partner. This blocks out some of the light and, from far away, the brighter star seems to fade. Astronomers call this an *eclipsing variable*.

Another type of star is the *pulsating variable*. It actually changes size. Astronomers think pressure inside the star builds up and pushes against its outer layers. So the star swells like a balloon, getting bigger and brighter. Then the star collapses in on itself,

getting smaller and dimmer until the next cycle begins.

Astronomers also classify exploding stars as variables, because the explosion produces a dramatic change in brightness. A *nova* is one type of exploding star. It can get thousands of times brighter in a matter of days or weeks and then slowly return to its former brightness. A nova explosion leaves the star basically still whole.

A *supernova* is a second, more violent type of exploding star. It can be a hundred times brighter than a nova. A supernova is fairly rare. But a large star at the end of its life span may explode this way. The entire outer shell of the star is blown off with tremendous force. The explosion packs the star's core into a dense ball of matter, possibly creating a pulsar. (*See* **pulsar.**)

See also **constellation.**

Supernova 1987A (left center) was first viewed in March 1987.
It was the brightest new object to appear in the sky for several centuries.

starfish

The starfish is not a fish. A better name for this animal is sea star, since it lives in the sea and is shaped like a star.

Most kinds of starfish have five arms around a central disk. But some starfish have as many as 50 arms. At the end of each arm is an eyespot that can sense light. If a starfish loses one of its arms, it can grow a new one.

Starfish are related to sea urchins. Both animals have tough, spiny skin and *tube feet*—tiny fingerlike parts. The tube feet of a starfish are in rows on the underside of each arm. Each tube foot has a sucker on the end. The starfish uses its tube feet to move along the bottom of the sea.

The starfish eats clams, oysters, and other mollusks. Its tube feet pull open the shells of these animals. The mouth of a starfish is on the underside of the central disk. After the tube feet have opened a shell, even only a crack, the starfish pushes part of its stomach out through its mouth and into the open shell. Digestive juices from the starfish's stomach kill, digest, and absorb the mollusk's soft body. When the meal is finished, the starfish draws in its stomach and walks off, leaving behind the empty mollusk shell.

A starfish moves slowly on its tube feet over rocks, sand, and shells.

Starfish come in shades of yellow, orange, red, blue, and green. They vary in size. Most are about 15 centimeters (6 inches) across.

Star-Spangled Banner

"The Star-Spangled Banner" is the national *anthem*—song—of the United States. It is played and sung at government ceremonies, political and social gatherings, and sporting events. The song has become recognized as a musical symbol of the United States. Americans rise and stand at attention whenever "The Star-Spangled Banner" is played. They do this to show their love and respect for their country.

Francis Scott Key, a young Maryland lawyer, wrote the words to "The Star-Spangled Banner" during the War of 1812. During this war between Britain and the United States, British ships sailed up Chesapeake Bay to attack the port of Baltimore, Maryland. An American doctor, William Beanes, had been captured and was being held prisoner on a British ship. Key and another American, John Skinner, were asked to talk to the British about freeing Beanes.

At the time, the British fleet stood just south of Fort McHenry, which protected the river route to Baltimore. The fort aimed its guns at any enemy ships that tried to reach Baltimore Harbor. As Key and Skinner boarded the ship that carried Beanes, the British fleet was about to begin bombarding Fort McHenry. The British intended to capture the fort so that the fleet could go on to Baltimore. They agreed to release Beanes, but decided to hold all three men until the battle was over. This way, the three Americans could not tell anyone the British plan.

On Tuesday, September 13, 1814, the attack began. It continued all day and into the night. Key became more and more fearful that Fort McHenry would fall to the British. He paced the deck through the long night. Explosions sent flashes of light through the darkness, but there was so much smoke that he could not tell which side was winning.

British ships bombard Fort McHenry. Francis Scott Key was being held on one of the ships. He kept looking to see if the Star-Spangled Banner was still flying over the fort.

When morning arrived, the smoke cleared for a moment. Key saw that the American flag still flew atop Fort McHenry. That told him that the British attack had failed. He reached into his pocket and took out an old envelope. On its back, he began writing the words of relief and joy that flooded his head. When the British released Key, he went ashore and wrote three more verses. A Baltimore newspaper printed them. Then an actor named Ferdinand Durang matched the words to the tune of a popular old English song, "To Anacreon in Heaven."

Now known as "The Star-Spangled Banner," the song began to be sung on patriotic occasions. Through the years, its popularity grew. Congress finally made it the national anthem in 1931.

THE STAR-SPANGLED BANNER
Oh! say, can you see,
by the dawn's early light,
What so proudly we hailed
at the twilight's last gleaming?
Whose broad stripes and bright stars,
thro' the perilous fight,
O'er the ramparts we watched
were so gallantly streaming?
And the rockets' red glare,
the bombs bursting in air,
Gave proof thro' the night
that our flag was still there.
Oh! say, does that star-spangled
banner yet wave
O'er the land of the free
and the home of the brave?

state government

Each of the 50 states in the United States has its own government. A state government is responsible for keeping order in that state and protecting its citizens.

The *federal*—national—government in Washington, D.C., decides matters that affect the entire United States. For example, only the federal government can coin money or declare war.

State governments have power over matters of local importance. A state's government is responsible for the state's school system. It also makes laws regarding voting, marriage, and divorce. State governments run social programs, build state highways, and have authority over the governments of the state's cities, towns, and villages. The Constitution of the United States outlines the different responsibilites of the national and state governments. (*See* **Constitution of the United States.**)

Despite differences in size and population, all of the states have governments with the same basic features. Each selects one of its cities as its *capital.* This is where the state government is located. Sometimes the capital is the largest city, such as Salt Lake City, Utah. But often it is a smaller, centrally located city, such as Springfield, Illinois.

Every state has a *constitution.* This is a written document that describes the different *branches*—parts—of the state government and how they work. The *legislative* branch consists of the state *legislature.* It is responsible for making the state's laws and setting taxes. Representatives to this law-making body are elected by the state's voters. Every state legislature except Nebraska's has two parts, called *houses.* The size of the legislature varies. Alaska, the biggest state, has one of the smallest legislatures, with only 60 members. New Hampshire, a small state, has the biggest legislature, with 424 members.

Every state has a *governor,* who is elected by the people. The governor is in charge of carrying out state laws. Different departments under the governor supervise such matters as farming, banking, education, and transportation. Together, the governor and the departments make up the *executive* branch of the state government.

The Texas state legislature is being addressed by the governor. Both the United States flag and the Texas flag fly above the platform.

The *judicial* branch of a state government usually consists of state courts. These courts make decisions in criminal cases and other legal arguments. The state's *supreme court* has power over all the other courts in the state.

See also **government** and **statehood**.

statehood

Statehood is full membership in a nation. In the United States of America, all 50 states have the same rights to govern their citizens and to take part in the national government in Washington, D.C. (*See* **state government**.)

The idea of creating an American nation made up of many states was set forth in the Declaration of Independence. Until that time, the 13 colonies along North America's Atlantic coast had been ruled by Britain. The declaration announced the colonists' decision to form "free and independent states."

As a result of the Revolutionary War, Britain gave the United States all the land north of the Ohio River and east of the Mississippi River. To encourage settlement in the area, Congress passed the Northwest Ordinance of 1787. This law listed the steps a new territory had to follow to become a state.

The first step was for Congress to name a governor and judges to rule the territory. When a territory had a population of 5,000 men, it could elect its own lawmaking body. It could also send a nonvoting representative to the United States Congress. When there was a total of 60,000 settlers in the territory, the territory could ask Congress for admission to the Union. Congress would then decide whether to admit the territory as a state. Each new state had the same rights as the older states.

Since the 13 colonies became states, 37 states have entered the Union by following these steps. The chart at right shows the order and year in which all 50 states joined the Union. The order and year for the first 13 states reflect the order and year in which each signed the Constitution.

STATES IN ORDER OF ADMISSION TO THE UNION

The Original 13 States

1. Delaware	Dec.	7, 1787
2. Pennsylvania	Dec.	12, 1787
3. New Jersey	Dec.	18, 1787
4. Georgia	Jan.	2, 1788
5. Connecticut	Jan.	9, 1788
6. Massachusetts	Feb.	6, 1788
7. Maryland	Apr.	28, 1788
8. South Carolina	May	23, 1788
9. New Hampshire	June	21, 1788
10. Virginia	June	25, 1788
11. New York	July	26, 1788
12. North Carolina	Nov.	21, 1789
13. Rhode Island	May	29, 1790

States Admitted Later

14. Vermont	Mar.	4, 1791
15. Kentucky	June	1, 1792
16. Tennessee	June	1, 1796
17. Ohio	Mar.	1, 1803
18. Louisiana	Apr.	30, 1812
19. Indiana	Dec.	11, 1816
20. Mississippi	Dec.	10, 1817
21. Illinois	Dec.	3, 1818
22. Alabama	Dec.	14, 1819
23. Maine	Mar.	15, 1820
24. Missouri	Aug.	10, 1821
25. Arkansas	June	15, 1836
26. Michigan	Jan.	26, 1837
27. Florida	Mar.	3, 1845
28. Texas	Dec.	29, 1845
29. Iowa	Dec.	28, 1846
30. Wisconsin	May	29, 1848
31. California	Sept.	9, 1850
32. Minnesota	May	11, 1858
33. Oregon	Feb.	14, 1859
34. Kansas	Jan.	29, 1861
35. West Virginia	June	20, 1863
36. Nevada	Oct.	31, 1864
37. Nebraska	Mar.	1, 1867
38. Colorado	Aug.	1, 1876
39. North Dakota	Nov.	2, 1889
40. South Dakota	Nov.	2, 1889
41. Montana	Nov.	8, 1889
42. Washington	Nov.	11, 1889
43. Idaho	July	3, 1890
44. Wyoming	July	10, 1890
45. Utah	Jan.	4, 1896
46. Oklahoma	Nov.	16, 1907
47. New Mexico	Jan.	6, 1912
48. Arizona	Feb.	14, 1912
49. Alaska	Jan.	3, 1959
50. Hawaii	Aug.	21, 1959

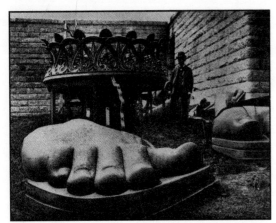

The torch and feet of the Statue of Liberty before the statue was put together.

Statue of Liberty

The Statue of Liberty is one of the United States' most beloved symbols. This huge statue of a woman, known as *Liberty Enlightening the World,* stands in New York Harbor, facing out to sea. Its raised right hand holds a torch, which represents the light of freedom. The left hand carries a book bearing the date of the Declaration of Independence—July 4, 1776.

The statue was a gift from France on the 100th birthday of the United States. The French people donated about $250,000 to pay for the statue. It was designed by the French sculptor Frédéric-Auguste Bartholdi. He planned a statue that would be 150 feet (45 meters) tall. The French engineer Gustave Eiffel—who later created the Eiffel Tower in Paris—designed an iron framework to support the statue. Thin sheets of copper were hammered into shape over a mold and then welded to the framework.

Work on the statue continued in Paris for ten years. On July 4, 1884, the completed statue was dedicated with a great celebration. The statue was then carefully taken apart, packed into 214 crates, and shipped to New York City.

The American people donated about $280,000 for the statue's *pedestal*—base. The granite-and-concrete pedestal was designed by Richard Morris Hunt and built on

Bedloe's Island, today known as Liberty Island. In 1886, the statue was placed atop the pedestal. The same year, it was dedicated by President Grover Cleveland. The pedestal brought the total height of the monument to over 300 feet (60 meters). In 1903, a poem by Emma Lazarus was added to the pedestal. The poem, "The New Colossus," includes these famous words: "Give me your tired, your poor, your huddled masses, yearning to breathe free. . . ."

During the late 1800s and early 1900s, millions of Europeans immigrated to the United States to start a new life. They crossed the Atlantic Ocean by boat. They knew they had reached the United States when they saw the Statue of Liberty. For most, it was a sight they would never forget.

The Statue of Liberty continues to hold special meaning for millions of people. The statue was repaired and rededicated to all Americans on its 100th birthday in 1986.

The Statue of Liberty stands on a stone pedestal in New York Bay.

steam engine

You have seen steam rising from boiling water, and heard it whistling through teakettle spouts. Expanding steam is also powerful enough to drive big engines. Most electric generators are driven by steam engines.

Power for a steam engine begins with a boiler. A boiler is like a giant kettle. When the water in it boils, much of it turns to a gas called *water vapor.* Steam is a mixture of water vapor and air. Steam takes up more space than water. There is not enough space in the boiler for the steam. So the steam pushes to get out.

There are two types of steam engines—*piston engines* and *turbines.* A piston engine is something like an automobile engine. Short rods—the pistons—move up and down in a hollow cylinder. The pistons are connected to a drive shaft. Steam pressure from the boiler pushes the pistons and makes them move. The moving pistons turn the drive shaft. Older railroad locomotives were powered by this kind of engine. On the outside of these locomotives, you could see the drive shaft moving the wheels. (*See* **engine.**)

Turbines are the engines used in electric power plants and most large ships. Turbines have large fanlike blades attached to one end of a drive shaft. When steam pressure from the boiler pushes against the blades, they turn at high speed and with great power.

The modern steam engine was patented in 1769 by James Watt, a Scottish inventor. Watt's idea was to heat water in a boiler apart from the engine. That made it easier to control steam pressure. Watt had other ideas that improved the steam engine.

The steam engine changed the way people lived and worked. It made modern industry possible. By 1800, steam engines were used to drive factory machinery such as looms, so goods could be produced more quickly. The steam engine also improved transportation. Ships and locomotives were powered with steam engines, which also aided in laying miles of railroad track.

Today, electric engines and oil-powered engines have replaced many steam engines. These engines are safer, quieter, and use less energy. But steam engines have not disappeared. They are still an important driving force in the modern world.

This electrical power plant burns coal to heat water until it becomes steam. The steam turns large turbines that generate electricity. Extra steam pours from the stacks.

steel

Steel is an alloy made of iron and a small amount of carbon. At high temperatures, the iron and carbon combine to create *cementite*. Cementite makes the steel harder and stronger than iron alone. Carbon also lowers the melting point of steel. If the alloy has too much carbon, it is not steel, but cast iron. (*See* **iron** and **alloy.**)

Steel may also contain various other elements, especially chromium, aluminum, nickel, or silicon. The additional elements are added to the steel to make it easier to form into beams, pipes, and sheets. They also help steel last longer by protecting it from rust and from other kinds of *corrosion* —weakening. (*See* **rust.**)

Steel can be stretched and pounded into thin sheets, which are then molded into car bodies and other objects. The steel frames of skyscrapers are strong enough to resist earthquakes, winds, and extreme changes in temperature. (*See* **steelmaking.**)

Low-alloy steel contains about one part carbon in a hundred, and up to five parts in

Workers build the framework for a power plant with steel beams and columns.

a hundred of other elements. These other elements may be chromium, nickel, tungsten, or titanium. Low-alloy steel is quite strong, and is used in construction and in many kinds of heavy machinery.

High-alloy steel contains larger amounts of the added elements. It is designed to withstand heat and corrosion better than other types of steel. *Stainless steel* is one type of high-alloy steel. It is used in jet engines, surgical tools, cooking utensils, and tableware—knives, forks, and spoons.

The greatest amount of steel is used for making automobiles. Most of the rest is used in construction and in making other machines. The Soviet Union, the United States, Japan, West Germany, and France are the world's leading producers of steel.

steelmaking

Steel is made by blending just the right amount of carbon with iron. Steel may also contain the elements tungsten, chromium, nickel, and titanium. (*See* **steel.**)

Steelmaking begins with mining *iron ore* —rock rich in iron. The iron ore is taken to a steel mill. There it is crushed and heated in

At left, a huge bucket pours melted iron ore into a furnace. Carbon and other minerals are added to the iron to produce steel. At right, the engine blocks for ship engines are cooling. Melted steel was poured into molds where it hardened into shape.

huge furnaces. When the ore melts, impurities are removed, and carbon and other elements are added. These elements give the steel different properties—such as greater strength, or better resistance to *corrosion* —weakening by chemicals.

Archaeologists have found steel objects that were made more than 3,000 years ago, during the Iron Age. People made this steel by melting iron ore and mixing in carbon from the charcoal fire. But it was difficult to control how much carbon mixed with the iron. Most metal objects continued to be made of iron.

In 1856, Sir Henry Bessemer developed a new way to make steel. This method is called the *Bessemer process.* Melted iron is poured into a pear-shaped furnace called a *Bessemer converter.* Air is forced into the converter through nozzles at the bottom. Oxygen in the air combines with excess carbon and impurities in the iron and escapes through the open top. The color of the flame at the mouth of the furnace tells workers when to turn off the air and when the steel

is ready. The Bessemer process made it possible to produce steel containing just enough carbon. Too much carbon made cast iron, not steel.

The *open-hearth process,* developed in 1857, further improved steelmaking. Larger amounts of steel could be processed at one time. The amount of gases added to the iron was measured more exactly. This produced steel of a more uniform composition. The high temperatures of the open-hearth process made it possible to melt down scrap iron and steel and use them again.

Later, the electric furnace was invented. It worked at temperatures as high as 2,000° C (3,600° F). This burned away more impurities and produced even better steel.

Today, steel is still produced by these three methods. But most modern steel mills use *oxygen furnaces.* These furnaces operate at nearly 2,200° C (4,000° F). The higher temperatures burn away even more impurities. Jets of steam and pure oxygen fired through the melted iron at very high speeds also burn off impurities.

Much steel is milled into sheets of various thicknesses. The glowing hot metal becomes a little thinner each time it is rolled through the mill.

The melted steel is poured into molds and shaped into bars, sheets, rods, or *ingots* —blocks. These go through various heat treatments to make the steel stronger. *Tempered steel* is heated, then quickly cooled in oil or water. The heating and cooling are repeated several times. *Annealed steel* is heated and allowed to cool gradually. Annealed steel is softer and easier to shape than tempered steel. *Case hardening* adds extra carbon, and produces steel with an extra-hard shell.

During production, steel is checked for air bubbles, cracks, and uniformity. After hardening, it is tested for strength and flexibility. Experts use electron microscopes, X rays, and spectroscopes to make sure the steel leaving the steel mill is of high quality.

Stevenson, Robert Louis

Robert Louis Stevenson was a writer whose books are loved by both children and adults. He is best known for his exciting stories of adventure. But Stevenson was sick most of his life, and did a lot of his writing in bed.

Stevenson was born in Edinburgh, Scotland, in November 1850. As a child, he suffered from tuberculosis, a lung disease that made him very weak. He loved to spend his time reading and often had to study at home instead of going to school. Stevenson began college at the age of 17. He earned a law degree, but never had a career as a lawyer. In his heart, he knew he wanted to be a writer. He began publishing short stories when he was about 25. At age 30, he married Fanny Osbourne, a divorced woman who had two children. They had a happy marriage.

Stevenson became famous after *Treasure Island* was published in 1883. It is the story of a boy named Jim Hawkins. Jim follows a pirate's map to the buried treasure of Captain Kidd. While looking for the treasure, Hawkins gets involved with pirates. The idea for the book came from a story Stevenson first told his wife's son.

Stevenson's second major book, *The Strange Case of Dr. Jekyll and Mr. Hyde*, appeared in 1886. This frightening story is about a scientist named Jekyll. His experiments turn him into an ugly, evil man called

Kidnapped

Dr. Jekyll
and Mr. Hyde

Treasure Island

Stevenson wrote exciting adventure stories and a collection of children's poems.

Mr. Hyde. That same year, Stevenson wrote *Kidnapped*, a book that many people consider his best. It is about the adventures of a young man who is kidnapped in order to keep him from inheriting an estate.

Stevenson also wrote many short stories and poems. *A Child's Garden of Verses* was published in 1885. This book is a collection of poems for children. It contains such favorites as "My Shadow," "The Swing," and "The Land of Counterpane."

Stevenson found that being near the sea made him feel better and seemed to improve his health. So in 1888, he and his family left home to travel around the Samoan Islands in the South Pacific Ocean. Stevenson built a large house on one of the islands and became active in the community. He died in 1894, at the age of 44, and was buried by the native Samoans. He had become their good friend.

stocks and bonds

Businesses raise money by selling stocks and bonds. Governments, too, sell bonds.

Stock is sold in *shares*. If you buy shares of a company's stock, you become one of the owners of the business. People who buy stock are called *shareholders* or *stockholders*. Shareholders receive *stock certificates* —documents telling how many shares they own. Companies owned by stockholders are called *corporations*.

Stockholders buy stock in the hope of making a profit from their investment. This can be done in two ways. They can sell the stock for more than what they paid for it. They can also collect *dividends*. Dividends are payments the company makes to its stockholders. The money for the dividends comes from the company's profits.

When people buy bonds, they are loaning money to whoever issued the bonds. People who own bonds are called *bondholders*. Their bonds *mature* on a specific date. This means that on the date of maturity, the issuer must repay the loan plus *interest*—a fee for using the loaned money. Receiving interest is one way people can make a profit from buying bonds. Another way is to sell the bonds to someone else at a higher price before they mature.

stomach

The stomach is a muscular organ in the upper left side of your belly. It is part of the digestive system and helps digest food. An adult's stomach can hold about 1.4 liters (3 pints) of food.

When you swallow food, it goes down a tube called the *esophagus* and enters your stomach. Muscles in the stomach wall churn the food, breaking it up and mixing it with stomach juices. The churning tends to begin around your usual mealtimes. You feel and hear it as "growling."

The stomach is lined with tiny glands. When there is food in your stomach, some of these glands release *enzymes*—substances that help digest food. One enzyme, pepsin, begins to digest proteins. Other glands release hydrochloric acid. This acid softens the food and destroys most of the bacteria in it. Solid food stays in your stomach for several hours while it is being digested.

A small muscle at the lower end closes off your stomach from the small intestine. When food is being digested in the stomach, this muscle is squeezed tight. When the stomach has completed its job, this muscle relaxes. Little by little, food passes into the small intestine to be digested further. (*See* **intestine.**)

See also **digestion** and **gland.**

The stomach is an organ in the upper abdomen that helps digest food.

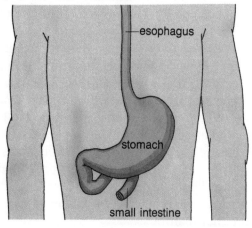

Stonehenge is an ancient ruin in England. It may have been built as an observatory.

stone, *see* rock

Stone Age, *see* man and woman, prehistoric

Stonehenge

Stonehenge is a mysterious ruin of stones and holes that lies on Salisbury Plain in southern England. Scientists believe that ancient peoples first started to build Stonehenge about 4,000 years ago.

Stonehenge today looks like a series of broken circles of enormous stones. The largest stones stand upright in pairs. Slabs of stone placed on top of the pairs form structures that look like giant doorways. At the center of Stonehenge, there is a flat stone about 16 feet (5 meters) long. It is called the Altar-Stone, but we do not know if it was used as an *altar*—a table for worship. Stones forming two horseshoe patterns surround the Altar-Stone. Outside of these, there are two circles of stones, three circles of holes, a bank of earth, and a ditch. The outer ditch forms a circle about 320 feet (96 meters) across.

The bank and ditch are broken at the northeast by an avenue lined with two pairs of ditches. Standing upright near the center

of the avenue is the Heel Stone, which is 16 feet (4.8 meters) tall. If you stand in the center of Stonehenge at sunrise on midsummer's day—the summer solstice—and look down the avenue, you will see the sun rise over the Heel Stone.

The stones used for the circles and horseshoes were all brought to Stonehenge from far away. The largest stones weigh as much as 50 tons (45 metric tons). They came from about 20 miles (32 kilometers) away, to the north. The smaller stones came from the western part of Wales, about 300 miles (480 kilometers) away. Scientists think the builders of Stonehenge used boats, sleds, strong ropes, and hundreds of men to move the heavy stones.

Some people think Stonehenge was built as a place for worshiping the sun or the moon. Others believe this stone monument was a burial site.

A study done in 1963 used a computer to figure out what could be seen from some of the stones. The study showed that certain stones and the spaces between them line up with the risings of the sun and moon at particular times of the year. Stonehenge may have been a calendar used to mark the seasons of the year.

Scientists are still carefully studying the stones, holes, and other remains at Stonehenge. They want to know how the monument once looked, who made it, and what it was used for.

Stone Mountain

Stone Mountain is a huge dome of hard rock, called *granite*. It stands over 700 feet (210 meters) tall and lies about 16 miles (26 kilometers) from Atlanta, Georgia. Carved in the side of the mountain are the figures of three southern heroes of the Civil War. Two of them are generals, Robert E. Lee and Thomas J. ("Stonewall") Jackson. The third is Jefferson Davis, president of the Confederate States of America.

Work on the Stone Mountain Memorial began in 1923. The sculptor Gutzon Borglum was hired to direct the carving of the figures. Borglum later left Stone Mountain to work on the gigantic Mount Rushmore Memorial in South Dakota. Another sculptor replaced Borglum and prepared a new design. In 1928, work stopped because there was not enough money to continue. (*See* **Rushmore, Mount.**)

The state of Georgia bought Stone Mountain and the land around it for a park in 1958. In 1964, the sculptor Walker Kirtland Hancock was hired to finish the memorial. It was finally completed in 1970.

See also **Civil War; Confederate States of America; Davis, Jefferson;** and **Lee, Robert E.**

The carving in Stone Mountain shows three southern heroes of the Civil War.

Dark, threatening clouds warn that a storm is coming. Animals and people seek shelter from the high winds, lightning, rain, and even hail brought by storms.

storm

A storm is a disturbance in the weather—the sky gets dark, the wind blows, and the rain or snow comes down. There are many kinds of storms. Some last only a few minutes, others last days. Some are gentle, others are fierce. Gentle storms are welcome because living things need the moisture they bring. But powerful storms can be frightening and cause great damage.

Kinds of Storms In some parts of the world, rains come so often that people scarcely think of them as storms. It may rain almost every day.

In drier parts of the world, rains come less often. When they do, there may be violent storms. In the Great Plains of North America, summer thunderstorms can bring high winds and very heavy rains. These storms also arrive with lightning and thunder—electrical bolts that can strike buildings or even people. Some rainstorms bring *hail* —hard balls of ice. A bad hailstorm can cause severe damage to crops. (*See* **lightning** and **hail.**)

Once in a while, strong thunderstorms may produce a *tornado*. A tornado is a small but extremely violent and dangerous storm. It can lift a car or even a house into the air.

Tornadoes have been seen in most parts of the United States east of the Rocky Mountains. But they are most frequent in the southern Great Plains. (*See* **tornado.**)

In mountain regions, storms can come up very suddenly. In the summer, there are many thunderstorms. Sometimes, the rain falls so heavily that the storm is called a "cloudburst" or a "gully washer." On steep mountainsides, the rain will run off very quickly. Mountain streams swell into rushing torrents that can cause sudden, severe floods.

In the winter, most of North America receives snowstorms. The most severe of these storms is called a *blizzard*. In a blizzard, the temperature is especially cold, the winds are very strong, and the snow falls very fast. The winds whip the falling snow into such a thick swirl that a person can see only a few feet ahead. (*See* **blizzard.**)

Tropical storms form over oceans near the equator. Those that form over the southeastern Atlantic are called *hurricanes*. They sometimes strike the southern and eastern United States. A hurricane can be hundreds of miles across, and may have winds of up to 320 kilometers (200 miles) per hour. Hurricanes are the most powerful storms on earth. (*See* **hurricane.**)

When cold air meets warm air, the warm air rises, and the cold air rushes in to take its place, causing wind. Moisture in the warm air condenses as it cools, causing rain.

How Storms Form Many storms are caused when air masses of different temperature and pressure run into each other. Warm, moist air often forms a mass of air that has low pressure. Cool, dry air forms a mass of air with high pressure. If you could look down on a low-pressure area in the northern hemisphere from a plane or satellite, you would see that its winds travel *counterclockwise*—in the opposite direction of a clock's hands. In a high-pressure area, the winds move clockwise. But south of the equator, in the southern hemisphere, the patterns are the opposite.

A *front* is where a low-pressure mass and a high-pressure mass meet. If the differences between the temperatures and pressures of the two masses are great, high winds and heavy rains may result.

The moisture in the low-pressure mass comes into contact with the cold air of the high-pressure mass. The moisture forms clouds of water vapor. If it cools further, it condenses, forming rain or snow. Storm activity often forms along a front.

Weather forecasters know of several ways to predict a storm. One signal is a drop in air pressure. Air pressure is measured by a *barometer*. Weather reports often include the *barometric pressure*. It is usually measured in inches of mercury. Pressure of 30 inches is normal for most regions near sea level. When the barometer falls rapidly, a large storm is likely to be approaching. At the end of a storm, the barometer begins to rise. This signals that the cool, dry air of a high-pressure mass is approaching and that skies will be clearing. (*See* **barometer.**)

Atmospheric pressure falls when a storm is approaching.

Another way to predict a storm is by wind direction. In most of North America, winds from the northwest mean good weather for the next 24 hours. When the wind swings around and comes from the southwest, rain is more likely. Along the New England shore, nasty storms come on northeast winds and are called "nor'easters."

See also **meteorology.**

The Strait of Gibraltar, a narrow waterway between Europe (above) and Africa (below).

strait

A strait is a narrow body of water that connects two large bodies of water. Like a natural canal, a strait allows water to pass from one large body of water to another. It also provides passage for ships and sea life. The same kinds of fish can be found living at both ends of a strait.

The Strait of Gibraltar, which connects the Mediterranean Sea and Atlantic Ocean, is very short. Other straits are long and twisting. One such strait, the Strait of Magellan, cuts across the southern end of South America from the Atlantic Ocean to the Pacific. It is 576 kilometers (360 miles) long.

Some straits are very narrow. The Bosporus, which connects the Black Sea with the Mediterranean, is less than 1.6 kilometers (1 mile) wide in places. But the Davis Strait, between Canada and Greenland in the North Atlantic Ocean, is as much as 320 kilometers (200 miles) wide. The Bering Strait, connecting the Bering Sea to the Arctic Ocean, is another wide strait. It separates Alaska from Siberia. The Bering Strait is about 57.6 kilometers (36 miles) wide.

Stravinsky, Igor

Many people consider Igor Stravinsky the most important composer of the 1900s. He was born in Russia near the city of St. Petersburg (now called Leningrad) in 1882. He studied law, and in his spare time, he studied music. He finally decided to become a musician instead of a lawyer.

As a young man, Stravinsky left Russia and settled in Paris, France. There he met another Russian, the great ballet director Sergei Diaghilev. Diaghilev asked him to write music for ballet. Stravinsky's first great composition, *The Firebird,* was written for Diaghilev's dance company.

Another of Igor Stravinsky's ballets, *The Rite of Spring,* was first performed in 1913. The music and the dancing were so shocking that the audience became very angry. They interrupted the performance and damaged the theater. Within a few years, however, people recognized *The Rite of Spring* as a great work of art. It has been played by orchestras ever since.

Stravinsky continued writing many kinds of music. In 1939, France was about to be invaded by German armies. Stravinsky moved to the United States and settled in California. He composed many new pieces and sometimes conducted major orchestras when they played his music. Stravinsky died in 1971.

stringed instrument, *see* musical instrument

stunt men and women

The stories in movies and on television are often filled with excitement and adventure. They may feature car chases, explosions, or people escaping from a burning building. Such scenes are too dangerous for actors and actresses to perform. Instead, stunt men and stunt women are hired as substitutes to create the scenes safely.

It takes special training to perform such dangerous acts. Some stunt men are experts at crashing cars without getting trapped inside them. Some stunt women know how to fall off a galloping horse without breaking an arm or leg.

A stunt man tumbles over a moving car (above). He uses gymnastic training to reduce the chances of injury. He also wears protective padding (below) for safety.

Stunt men and women must look like the actors and actresses for whom they are substituting. For example, a young, thin stunt man with curly black hair would not be a good substitute for an older, heavier actor with white hair.

Movies and television shows are seldom filmed the way you see them, from beginning to end. All scenes taking place at one location may be filmed together. The dangerous scenes requiring stunt work are filmed at one time, too. All these scenes are later put in the proper order in the film.

If a movie includes a scene where a young woman jumps from a moving train, a stunt woman is filmed performing the jump. The actress who plays the part of the young woman is filmed standing on the train as if she were about to jump. Then she is filmed rolling on the ground near the train as if she has just jumped. When these scenes are later put together, the stunt woman's face will not be clearly visible. It will be hard to see that the actress did not perform the jump.

Stunt men and women usually are not hurt performing even the most difficult acts.

They plan all their stunts carefully and practice them over and over again. They also check carefully to make sure that any equipment they need to use is in good condition. Yet things sometimes do go wrong, so stunt work can be dangerous.

Only about 100 men and women make a living doing stunts. Most work in Hollywood, where most movies and television shows are made.

See also **movie** and **actors and acting.**

submarine

A submarine is a boat that can travel underwater as well as on the surface. Most submarines are used for war, but some are used for scientific research.

Early Submarines The first submarine was built in 1620 by a Dutch inventor named Cornelis Drebbel. It was made of a wooden frame covered with greased leather and powered by people rowing. They used oars that extended through the sides. Leather flaps covered the oar holes so water could not come in when the vessel *submerged*—went underwater. This craft, and similar ones designed by Drebbel, traveled under the surface of the Thames River in England between 1620 and 1624.

The first submarine used in war was the *Turtle.* It was built by a college student named David Bushnell and was used during the American Revolution. It was about 2 meters (7½ feet) high and 1.7 meters (5½ feet) wide, and shaped like a walnut standing on end. It was made of wood and powered by foot-operated propellers. The *Turtle* submerged and surfaced by pumping water into and out of a tank inside the submarine. The craft carried a compass, a depth indicator, and a breathing tube that could be used like a skin diver's snorkel.

The *Turtle*—a one-person submarine—was tried out during the Revolutionary War.

The *Turtle* was designed to tow an explosive underwater and attach it to the hull of an enemy ship. One night in 1776, Ezra Lee, a sergeant in the Revolutionary Army, tried to get the *Turtle* to attach the explosive to the hull of a British warship, the *Eagle.* After several failures, Lee released the charge and left. It exploded without damaging the *Eagle.*

Before building his famous steamboat, Robert Fulton experimented with submarines for several years. The submarine *Nautilus* was completed by Fulton in 1801. It was made of iron ribs covered with sheets of copper. It was a little over 6 meters (21 feet) long and about 2 meters (6½ feet) across its widest point. The *Nautilus* was the first submarine to use *diving planes.* Diving planes are horizontal rudders that can guide a submarine up and down.

The *Nautilus* submerged by taking water into tanks. It contained enough air to support four men for three hours while submerged. Later, a tank of compressed air was added. This allowed the submarine to stay underwater for longer periods. The *Nautilus* carried out several successful tests, but never actually sank a ship in combat.

During the Civil War, the Confederate navy used submarines against Union blockades. The C.S.S. *Hunley* became the first submarine to sink an enemy ship. The *Hunley* was about 18 meters (60 feet) long and carried nine men—a navigator and eight men to turn the crankshaft. On February 17, 1864, the *Hunley* rammed an explosive into the side of a Union warship, the *Housatonic.* The *Housatonic* sank, but the explosion also sank the *Hunley.*

Submarines in the World Wars By the time of World War I (1914 to 1918), submarines were powered by diesel engines when on the surface and electric motors while submerged. Unlike diesel engines, electric motors and batteries do not need oxygen to operate. A submarine's diesel engines were also used to recharge the batteries that ran the electric motors.

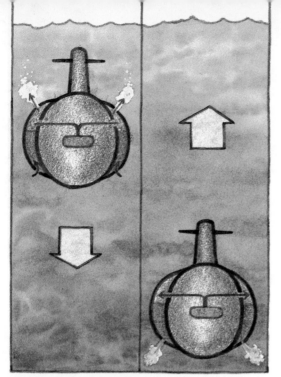

A submarine submerges by taking water into its ballast tanks. It surfaces by blowing compressed air into the tanks. This forces the water out.

Most World War I submarines were small—about 60 meters (200 feet) long—and were used mainly along coastlines. They had deck guns and *torpedoes*—underwater missiles. German submarines, called *U-boats,* proved to be deadly weapons. Some submarines were used for laying underwater *mines* —explosives that blow up when bumped.

During World War II (1939 to 1945), submarines were equipped with sonar to detect things underwater. Submarines were used on all the oceans of the world. Germany, Japan, and the United States all had large submarine fleets. Germany's U-boats were very effective against the Allies' shipping, especially at the beginning of the war. But by the last two years of the war, Allied destroyers had succeeded in stopping most U-boat damage. U.S. submarines were used mainly in the war against Japan, in the Pacific.

The modern submarine has a double hull. The inner hull—the *pressure hull*—can withstand very high pressures. This makes it possible for the submarine to go deep underwater and not be crushed by the water's weight. Between the two hulls are the fuel and *ballast* tanks. To dive, a submarine lets water into the ballast tanks. To surface, air is pumped into the ballast tanks, forcing the water out. Submarines have advanced kinds of radar and sonar, along with other modern equipment. Often, submarines cruise a little below the surface of the ocean, with their *periscopes* up so that they can see above the surface. A periscope is basically a long tube with two mirrors, positioned so that the viewer can see around corners or into the distance.

Nuclear Submarines On January 17, 1955, the first nuclear-powered submarine, the U.S.S. *Nautilus,* started its first voyage.

A nuclear submarine of the U. S. Navy. It can stay underwater for weeks because nuclear fuel does not need oxygen to burn.

A suburb has houses, schools, and stores. Many people who live in suburbs travel by car and work in a nearby city or town.

A nuclear-powered submarine can stay submerged for months at a time. This is because a nuclear reactor does not need air to produce power. Most U.S. nuclear submarines are designed to find and destroy other submarines. Some of them carry ballistic missiles that can be fired at land targets thousands of miles away.

See also **missile** and **warship.**

subtraction, *see* arithmetic

suburb

A suburb is a community located near a big city. Many suburbs began as places for city workers and their families to live. A city and its suburbs make up a *metropolitan area.* The United States has more than 25 metropolitan areas with over 1.5 million people.

A big city may have over a hundred suburbs. Added together, the suburbs may have a larger population than the city itself. New York City, for example, has about 7 million people. Its many suburbs have a total population of over 10½ million.

Suburbs have probably existed as long as there have been cities. Outside the ruins of ancient cities, scientists have found the remains of what seem to be large suburban homes. Modern suburbs had their start in the 1800s, during the Industrial Revolution. This was a time when factories were built in many cities. As a result, the cities became

crowded with people. At the same time, the factories produced smoke and noise that made cities unpleasant places to live. (*See* **Industrial Revolution.**)

Many people moved to suburbs, where there was more space and cleaner air. In the suburbs, a family could live in their own home with a yard. Suburban schools were often better than city schools. There was less crime in the suburbs, too.

By the late 1800s and early 1900s, suburbs had grown up around most American cities. Many of the people who lived in these suburban areas *commuted* to jobs in the city. This means they traveled to work on railroads, electric streetcars, or subways. Individual suburbs did not grow very large because most people wanted to live within walking distance of the train stations.

Beginning in the 1950s, Americans who lived in suburbs depended more and more on their own cars. Gasoline was cheap, and many new highways were built. The suburban population grew much larger and spread out. By 1970, more Americans lived in suburbs than in central cities.

Suburbs now depend much less than they used to on the cities they surround. Suburbs have big shopping malls. Many companies have moved to the suburbs. In most metropolitan areas, over half the suburban workers work in the suburbs, not in the city. In fact, many city dwellers now commute to jobs in the suburbs.

See also **city.**

subway

A subway is an underground railroad that provides speedy public transportation in a large city. Some subway systems also have stretches of aboveground track. Travel by subway can be much faster than travel by car or bus.

The first subway began operating in 1863 in London. It was called the *underground,* and used steam-powered locomotives. These produced a great deal of noise and smoke in the tunnels and in the subway cars. The electric locomotive was invented in 1881. It was quiet and produced no smoke. Soon, electric subway systems were being built in many large cities. Paris, Moscow, New York, Tokyo, and Toronto are just a few of the cities with subways.

In the United States, the first subway opened in Boston in 1897. A New York City subway system opened in 1904. These two subway systems have been expanded over the years. The New York City system is the largest in the world. It has more than 390 kilometers (238 miles) of track and carries millions of passengers each day. Chicago, Philadelphia, Washington, D.C., and San Francisco also have subway systems.

Today's subways are electrically powered. The electric current, in almost all systems, is direct current. It comes from generators that may be many miles away. The current is carried by a "third rail" running beneath one of the wheel rails or between the rails.

People called *dispatchers* control subway traffic. Large control boards show the locations and speeds of all the trains. The dispatchers can communicate with train operators, switch trains from one track to another, and cut off power in emergencies. Their tasks are made easier by computers. The Bay Area Rapid Transit (BART) system in San Francisco can be run completely by computer.

Subways are being improved in other ways, too. Subway cars in Moscow, Paris, and Montreal have rubber wheels, instead of metal, to reduce noise. Experts are always seeking ways to improve subway safety.

Below, an underground subway station. Left, a subway sometimes travels aboveground.

Sudan

Capital: Khartoum
Area: 967,495 square miles (2,505,812 square kilometers)
Population (1985): about 22,972,000
Official language: Arabic

The Sudan is a large nation in northeastern Africa. It borders Ethiopia, Kenya, Uganda, Zaire, the Central African Republic, Chad, Libya, Egypt, and the Red Sea. The Blue Nile, White Nile, and Nile rivers flow north through the Sudan.

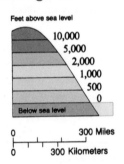

Feet above sea level

10,000
5,000
2,000
1,000
500
0

Below sea level

0   300 Miles
0   300 Kilometers

The Sudan has three main regions. The hot, rainy southern region has rain forests and one of the largest swamp areas in the world. The drier central region is mostly grassland. The north has the hot, sandy Nubian and Libyan deserts. In some years, parts of these deserts receive no rain.

Most Sudanese people live near the Nile. The river provides transportation and a link to the Mediterranean Sea. It is also the main source of water. Irrigated fields line the Nile, and Sudan's two largest cities—Khartoum and Omdurman—are on its banks.

About three-fourths of the Sudan's people work as farmers. They grow peanuts, sesame, cassava, corn, rice, dates, cotton, and melons. The juicy melons provide water during the dry season. Gum arabic from acacia trees is sold to other countries for making perfumes and candy.

The Sudan also has *nomads*—people who move from place to place. Nomads and their herds of cattle or camels roam the deserts and grasslands seeking water and food.

Black Africans live in the south. They follow traditional African religions or Christianity. People in the grasslands and desert are related to the ancient Egyptians, Arabs, and Nubians—an ancient group of black Africans. Almost all northerners are Muslims—followers of Islam. They make up the majority of the population.

Around 2000 B.C., the Nubians set up the kingdom of Kush in the Sudan. The Nubians learned to work with iron, and they traded gold, ivory, and slaves with Egypt. Kush may

Sudanese workers stack mud bricks that have dried in the sun.

have been destroyed by Axum, another Sudanese kingdom, around A.D. 350. (*See* **African civilizations.**)

Arab Muslims invaded the Sudan around 1100. They were followed by other Muslim groups. Egyptians took control of the region in 1821. The Sudanese regained control, but lost it again to Egypt and Britain in 1898. After years of struggle, the Sudan became an independent nation in 1956. Independence was followed by civil war between the southern and northern Sudanese. A treaty signed in 1972 gave the southern Sudanese more power in governing their own affairs.

Suez Canal, *see* canal

sugar

Sugar is a natural product that makes foods taste sweet. Both sugar and starch are members of the food group called *carbohydrates.* Carbohydrates are the body's main sources of energy. (*See* **carbohydrate.**)

Most sugar is made by green plants, by a process called *photosynthesis.* When their leaves are exposed to sunlight, the energy of the sun makes water and carbon dioxide combine to form sugar. The sugar is then stored in the roots and stems of the plant. (*See* **photosynthesis.**)

Kinds of Sugar The sugar made by green plants is called *glucose.* Honey and sweet fruits contain large amounts of glucose. Unlike other foods, glucose does not have to be *digested*—broken down—by your body. Instead, it is absorbed directly into your bloodstream, where it is known as *blood sugar.*

Fructose is found in fruits and vegetables. It is also called *fruit sugar* or *levulose.* The sugar we use at the table is *sucrose.* Sucrose comes from sugarcane and sugar beets. It is one of the sugars that sweeten maple syrup. *Lactose* is a sugar found in milk. Sucrose and lactose are combinations of several different sugars. Sucrose, for example, can be broken down into glucose and fructose.

Sugar is a natural ingredient of milk, honey, fruit, and vegetables.

Using Sugar Many people like to add sugar to their food. They sprinkle it on cereal and fruit. They spoon it into tea and coffee. It is also added to jellies, jams, soft drinks, ice cream, baked goods, and many other packaged foods. It adds flavor and helps preserve the foods. Lactose is added to medicine tablets and capsules.

Sugar has other uses, too. It is an ingredient in dye and in some cosmetics. It is used as a preservative for tobacco. Sugarcane fibers are used to produce nylons and other plastics, and may even be part of your phonograph records! Most people can get enough sugar by eating fruits, vegetables, and grains. When you eat more sugar than you need for energy, your body turns the extra sugar into fat. Doctors often warn their patients to eat less sugar. Large amounts of sugar can cause cavities in teeth and other health problems. People with the disease called *diabetes* must be very careful about how much sugar they eat. (*See* **diabetes.**)

Sugar from Sugarcane Most of the sugar in the world comes from sugarcane and sugar beets. Sugarcane belongs to the grass family. It thrives in areas where there is warm weather, rich soil, and plenty of rainfall. Brazil, India, Cuba, Mexico, and China are among the world's leading growers of sugarcane. In the United States, sugarcane is grown mostly in Hawaii, Florida, and Louisiana.

Refined sugar is made from sugarcane (above) and from sugar beets (right).

The tall, thick stems of sugarcane hold large amounts of liquid sucrose. The stalks may grow as high as 15 feet (5 meters). When ready, they are harvested by hand or by machine.

After harvesting, the cane is taken to sugar factories for processing. The stalks are washed and cut. Next, a machine squeezes the cane to force out a sweet liquid called *cane juice.* The cane juice is filtered to be sure it is pure. Then it is heated to remove the water and turn the juice into a thick syrup. Heating continues until the sugar in the syrup forms crystals. The syrup is spun at a high speed in a round drum to separate the crystals. The crystals are *raw sugar.* The syrup that is spun off is *molasses.* Raw sugar is dissolved in water and goes through the whole filtering and spinning process again to make *refined sugar.* Any syrup remaining after the third round of processing is made into *brown sugar.*

White sugar is raw sugar that has been completely refined to remove everything except the sucrose. Some white sugar is pressed into cubes. Some is made into *confectioner's sugar*—powdered sugar. It is dusted over cakes and used to make icings and candies.

Sugar from Sugar Beets Sugar beets grow in areas with a temperate climate. The roots of these plants contain large amounts of sucrose. After harvesting, the sugar beets are sliced into thin strips and soaked in hot water. The sugar from the beets mixes with the hot water to form a sweet syrup. The syrup is then strained, boiled, and dried to form sugar. The Soviet Union, France, and the United States are among the world's leading growers of sugar beets.

History of Sugar Sugarcane was grown thousands of years ago in India and the islands of the South Pacific Ocean. China began to grow sugarcane around 100 B.C. Europeans began planting sugarcane in the 600s. Explorers and settlers from Spain and Portugal introduced sugarcane plants to Africa, Brazil, and the islands of the Caribbean Sea. Missionaries brought sugarcane to Louisiana in the 1750s.

The peoples of ancient Egypt, Greece, and Babylonia grew sugar beets over 2,000 years ago. During the 1800s, people learned to make sugar from the beets. Sugar factories—called *refineries*—spread across Europe. The first sugar-beet refinery in the United States was built near Oakland, California, in the 1830s.

sulfur

Sulfur is a yellow element that is not a metal. Eggs, cabbage, and onions contain sulfur compounds. Our bodies use sulfur compounds to form skin, hair, nails, and muscle.

Pure sulfur is found in rock deposits called *brimstone.* Natural sulfur compounds exist in rock formations, coal, and natural gas.

Each year, we use up about 63 billion kilograms (70 billion tons) of sulfur. Four-fifths of this total is used to make sulfuric acid. About half of the acid is mixed with phosphate rock to make a powerful fertilizer. Sulfur and sulfuric acid are also used in the production of insecticides, plastics, matches, explosives, paper, dyes, and steel. Sulfur is an important ingredient in medicines called *sulfa drugs.* Rubber must be treated with sulfur to remain useful at both low and high temperatures. (*See* **Goodyear, Charles** and **rubber.**)

When sulfur combines with oxygen in even small amounts, it pollutes the air, causing *acid rain.* Acid rain can kill fish, erode stone statues and buildings, and injure trees or crops. Since most coal and oil contain sulfur, the burning of coal and oil contributes to air pollution.

Sumer

Sumer was an ancient land of western Asia. It lay at the southern end of Mesopotamia—the region between the Euphrates and Tigris rivers. Today, this land is part of Iraq.

Sumer was settled around 3500 B.C.— about 5,500 years ago. The Sumerian people developed an advanced way of living, which we call *civilization.* They were among the first people to build cities and to invent a form of writing. Many of their inventions were used later by people who lived nearby.

Sumerian writing consisted of wedge-shaped marks that were pressed into wet clay tablets. This writing is called *cuneiform*—from a Latin word meaning "wedge."

This Sumerian statue has cuneiform writing on its robe.

Thousands of cuneiform tablets have survived. Many are business records, but some tell about Sumerian kings. Others set down the oldest written laws we know of, and even some songs.

The Sumerians knew how to make bronze. They watered their crops by irrigation. They fought from chariots and sailed ships south to the Persian Gulf. The Sumerians made bricks from baked clay and built huge temples and palaces. The walls of Uruk, one Sumerian city, were 18 feet (5.4 meters) thick and 6 miles (9.6 kilometers) long.

Sumer was weakened by invasions and by civil wars. About 1760 B.C., the ruler Hammurabi united Sumer with Babylonia. (*See* **Babylonia.**)

summer, *see* season

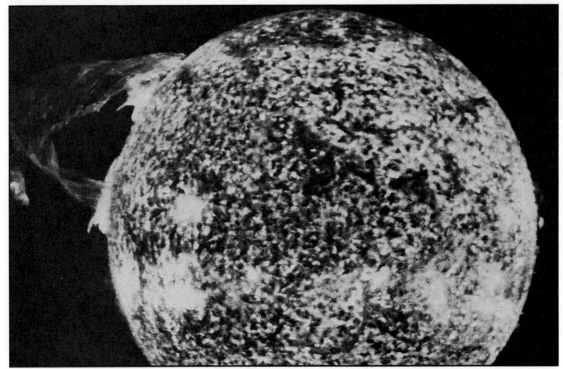

A photo from the Skylab telescope in space shows a large solar flare (left).
This region of swirling gas is wider than the distance from Earth to the moon!

sun

The sun is the star at the center of our solar system. Compared to other stars in the universe, our sun is about average in size and brightness. Yet without it, there would be no life on Earth.

Astronomers believe the sun is 1,392,000 kilometers (865,000 miles) across. That is more than 109 times larger than Earth. The sun also has much more mass than Earth—about 333,000 times more. The sun is so enormous that its gravity is strong enough to hold the planets in their orbits. Without such a strong pull on them, the planets would fly off into space. Most of the sun's tremendous mass consists of hydrogen and helium gases under great pressure. The sun contains three times as much hydrogen as helium. Only a small fraction of its mass is made up of other substances.

The sun is part of a huge *galaxy*—group of stars—called the Milky Way. The whole galaxy, including the sun and the planets that orbit it, is *rotating*—turning—around the galaxy's center at a very high speed. (*See* **Milky Way.**)

Like other stars, the sun is very hot and gives off huge amounts of heat and light. Temperatures at the sun's visible surface are about 5,510° C (9,950° F). They are much hotter deep inside the sun, where the heat is produced.

At the very core of every star, there is a kind of nuclear furnace. That furnace forces hydrogen atoms to unite and form helium atoms. When the centers of two atoms unite, this is called *nuclear fusion*. Nuclear fusion produces tremendous amounts of heat. Temperatures at the star's core can reach millions of degrees. The heat at the center gradually rises to the star's outer surface, making it very hot and bright. The star shines and sends out a steady flow of heat.

All that heat and light radiates outward. A small part of it reaches the planets in our solar system, but the sun is not hot enough to warm the outer planets very much. The sun's light also grows faint that far out in the solar system. Planets closer to the sun receive an abundance of heat and light. Mercury, the closest planet, gets so much sun that its sunlit side reaches a sizzling 510° C (950° F). But Earth receives just the right

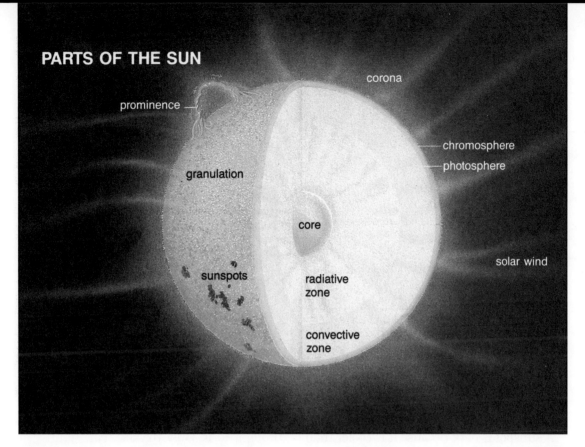

PARTS OF THE SUN

prominence

corona

granulation

chromosphere

photosphere

core

solar wind

sunspots

radiative
zone

convective
zone

amount of light and heat for living things to survive.

Inside the Sun Scientists believe that the sun's core is about 400,000 kilometers (249,000 miles) across. There, nuclear reactions produce temperatures that are as high as 10,000,000° C (18,000,000° F).

Surrounding the core is a thick layer of densely packed hydrogen and helium. Heat from the sun's core slowly passes through this layer on its way to the surface.

When we see pictures of the sun's surface, we are seeing the *photosphere.* It is an outer layer, about 480 kilometers (300 miles) thick. Heat from inside the sun passes through it. The photosphere is not smooth. It has a slightly grainy appearance that astronomers call *granulation.* There are about 4 million grains covering the sun at any one time. Astronomers have discovered that each grain is the top of a gas cloud. A cloud starts out small, and in less than ten minutes it spreads to almost 1,600 kilometers (1,000 miles) across. Soon, the cloud fades, only to be replaced by another new cloud.

Sunspots are dark patches that appear on the sun's surface. The patches vary in size

from hundreds of kilometers across to several times Earth's diameter. (*See* **sunspot.**)

The next layer above the photosphere is the *chromosphere.* The gases in this layer are transparent, and they are about 4,800 kilometers (3,000 miles) thick. They thin out toward the top. One unusual feature of this layer is that temperatures rise sharply in it. They go from 4,500° C (8,000° F) at the bottom of the chromosphere to 1,000,000° C (1,800,000° F) at the top.

Above the photosphere is the *corona*—the sun's outer layer. This layer has very thin gas and extends outward for tens of thousands of kilometers. The corona is even hotter than the chromosphere. It gets up around 2,000,000° C (3,600,000° F). This intense heat causes a steady stream of charged particles—mainly protons and electrons—to flow out into space. Astronomers call this stream of particles the *solar wind.*

See also **star** and **solar system.**

sunspot

A sunspot is a disturbance on the surface of the sun. To us, sunspots appear as dark

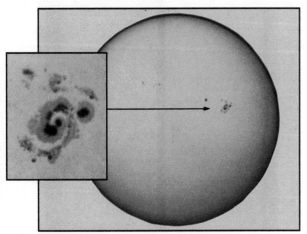

This sunspot (enlarged at left) has an unusual spiral shape. Most are round.

patches on the sun. The Chinese first noticed sunspots thousands of years ago. Today, we are still trying to learn what causes them.

A sunspot is dark because it is cooler than the surrounding surface. We also know that a sunspot has a very strong *magnetic field* —the area around it where the force of magnetism is felt. The smallest sunspots are hundreds of miles across. A large sunspot may cover an area many times larger than the earth! They often appear in pairs. A sunspot generally has a solid, dark center. Radiating out from the center are dark, hairlike lines that look like spokes on a wheel.

Old sunspots are always disappearing and new ones are always appearing. Their number changes from year to year in a regular pattern. From a year of low activity, sunspots increase in number for about five and a half years. Then they decrease for about five and a half years, reaching a new low. This 11-year pattern is called the *sunspot cycle.*

Sunspots affect radio transmissions on Earth, and also have something to do with the appearance of the northern lights. Some scientists think they may affect long-term weather patterns. (*See* **northern lights.**)

Superior, Lake, *see* Great Lakes

Supreme Court, United States

The U.S. Supreme Court is the nation's most important court. Its nine judges have the final say in all cases involving the U.S. Constitution. The Supreme Court is the highest court of the *federal*—national—court system. The federal courts form the *judicial branch* of the federal government.

The Supreme Court consists of a chief justice and eight associate justices. The justices are appointed by the president and approved by the Senate. They serve for life or until they retire.

Almost all cases that come before the Supreme Court have been tried in a lower court. The losing side in a trial may *appeal* —ask a higher court, such as the Supreme Court, to reconsider the decision. The Supreme Court does not have to hear every case brought to it. Only the Supreme Court can rule on a case involving one of the states, or when a foreign diplomat is concerned.

Many Supreme Court decisions have helped to explain the meaning of the Constitution. For example, the Constitution says that Congress must not make any laws that restrict free speech. In the 1960s, some students in Des Moines, Iowa, wore armbands to school to protest the Vietnam War. The school sent the protesters home. The students took the school to court. They said that wearing armbands was a form of speech, and that they should be allowed to wear them. The Supreme Court heard the case on appeal, and agreed with the students. Its decision gave broader meaning to the word *speech.*

The Supreme Court has the power to decide whether presidential actions and the laws of the states and Congress are *unconstitutional.* An unconstitutional law or action conflicts with the Constitution. A law or action that is declared unconstitutional can no longer be enforced.

In 1954, the Supreme Court found a state law in Kansas unconstitutional. Kansas used to have *segregated* schools—separate

The Supreme Court Building, where the court meets and hears cases. A left, the nine justices.

schools for black children and for white children. Black parents appealed to the Supreme Court to end this system. The Court decided that segregated schools could never be equal. It also said that having segregated schools went against a statement in the Constitution that promises everyone "equal protection of the laws." This decision had important effects. Many other states also had segregated schools, and all of them were forced to change their laws.

See also **government; Constitution of the United States;** and **Marshall, John.**

surfing

Surfing is the sport of riding ocean waves. The surfer stands on a long, flat *surfboard*. Powerful ocean waves carry the surfboard and its rider to shore. Surfing is a challenging and sometimes dangerous sport that is exciting to watch.

Surfboards are usually 6 to 7 feet (1.8 to 2 meters) long and about 2 feet (0.6 meter) wide. Most are made of fiberglass, a lightweight material that allows them to float on the water. Before starting a ride, the surfer must paddle out to where the waves just begin to form. Then the surfer points the board toward shore and waits for the right wave. The surfer "catches" a wave just as it begins to lift the board. The surfer lies facedown on the surfboard, paddles a few strong strokes toward shore, and then stands up. The force

A surfer rides in the curl of a wave as it breaks toward the beach.

of the wave takes over and carries the surfboard forward.

Surfers must have good balance and quick reactions. Expert surfers can make fancy turns while riding a wave by shifting their weight on the board. Surfers must be good swimmers, because falls from the board happen often.

Surfing is thought to have started in Hawaii more than 200 years ago. The sport is still enjoyed there. It is also popular in many other places, including southern California and Australia.

surgery

Many illnesses can be treated with medicines or bed rest. Some cases require surgery—the repair, removal, or replacement of diseased or damaged parts of the body. A *surgeon*—a doctor who performs surgery —may operate in a doctor's office or a hospital. Surgeons also treat people who have been injured in accidents or born with physical problems. Often, several surgeons perform surgery together, as a team, along with assistants and nurses.

A hundred years ago, surgery was seldom successful. It was often very painful, because doctors had not yet discovered ways to stop pain. Doctors and nurses did not know that to prevent the spread of infections, everything handled during an operation had to be very clean. Until they learned these things, surgeons often unknowingly made their patients worse instead of better. Death rates from surgery were very high. Therefore, people avoided surgery, unless they were already near death.

Surgery today is much safer. It was improved first by the development of *anesthetics*—substances to block pain. The second improvement was the discovery that germs caused infection. This led to the use of *antiseptics*—things that kill microorganisms that cause diseases. New medicines and procedures have made all medical treatments, including surgery, more successful. Blood

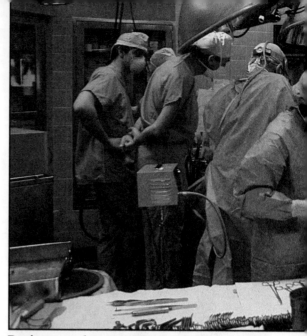

During open-heart surgery, a dozen or more doctors, nurses, and technicians work together in the operating room.

banks make blood available to patients who have lost a lot of their own blood. Today, when a patient has an operation, there is very good reason to look forward to his or her recovery.

Many young people have surgery to remove their infected tonsils or adenoids. The appendix is also removed when it becomes infected. The body does not need these parts, and surgery to remove them is very safe.

Most surgeons today specialize in doing particular types of surgery. *Orthopedic surgeons* repair and correct bones and joints. *Neurosurgeons* work with the brain and spinal cord. *Plastic surgeons* are experts in rebuilding injured or poorly formed parts of the body. *Cardiac surgeons* repair the heart and blood vessels. *Oral surgeons* remove teeth and rebuild jawbones.

An *organ transplant* is one of the most remarkable kinds of surgery. In this operation, the patient's diseased organ is removed. It is replaced by a healthy organ taken from a person who has just died. Kidneys, hearts, lungs, livers, and other organs have been successfully transplanted.

See also **anesthetic.**

Suriname, *see* **South America**

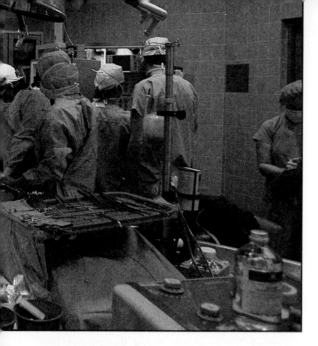

Sutter's Mill

Sutter's Mill was a sawmill in the Sacramento Valley of California. Gold was discovered there on January 24, 1848.

The mill was on property that belonged to John Augustus Sutter. Sutter had grown up in Switzerland. He settled in California in 1839 and started a colony called New Helvetia, which means "New Switzerland." California still belonged to Mexico, and Sutter was a Mexican citizen. Sutter became a prosperous farmer, trapper, and trader.

Only nine days before California became part of the United States, James Marshall, a carpenter who was building a mill for Sutter, discovered gold in a stream. The two men tried to keep it a secret, but word leaked out. Soon, thousands of gold-seekers were rushing to California, hoping to find their own riches. (*See* **Gold Rush.**)

Sutter's claim to his land under U.S. law was questioned. He could not keep prospectors from swarming all over his property. Within four years, all his money was gone. So were his dreams for New Helvetia. Sutter spent the rest of his life trying to get the state or U.S. government to pay him for the loss of his land. He died in 1880.

Today, a model of Sutter's Mill stands in Marshall Gold Discovery Historical Park at Coloma, California.

Swaziland, *see* Africa; South Africa

Sweden, *see* Scandinavia; Europe

sweetener, artificial

An artificial sweetener may be used to sweeten soft drinks, chewing gum, desserts, and other processed foods. It takes the place of natural sweeteners, such as sugar and honey. The two most commonly used artificial sweeteners in the United States are *saccharin* and *aspartame.* Saccharin is made from petroleum and coal products. Aspartame is made from plant substances.

Unlike sugar, artificial sweeteners are not carbohydrates, and they do not supply the body with energy. They are used mostly by people who want to lose weight or who have *diabetes,* a disease that prevents the body from using and storing sugar properly.

The use of artificial sweeteners in the United States is controlled by the U.S. government's Food and Drug Administration (FDA). The FDA studies artificial sweeteners to find out if they are safe. In 1970, it outlawed an artificial sweetener called *cyclamate.* FDA tests showed that cyclamate caused cancer in animals, but there was no proof that it caused cancer in people.

Other countries have their own laws about artificial sweeteners. In Canada, it is forbidden to add saccharin to processed foods. Some countries permit the use of sweeteners that are outlawed in the United States.

swimming

Swimming is a form of exercise enjoyed by many people. It is also a competitive sport. People swim in lakes, rivers, oceans, and pools. A person who swims well can take part in boating and other water sports, such as water skiing, diving, and scuba diving. (*See* **diving.**)

There are many ways to swim. You may lie facedown in the water, or on your back or side. You may also use a variety of arm and leg movements to move through the water. The movements are timed to go with your breathing.

Swimming lessons are given at schools, athletic clubs, and public pools. Organizations such as the Scouts, the Red Cross, and the "Y" also give lessons. Beginning swimmers first learn to float in the water. Then they learn the basic ways to kick their legs and move their arms. They must get used to timing their breathing. Sometimes they do this by bobbing up and down in the water. When they come up, they take a breath. When they go back under, they let the breath out. Beginning swimmers also learn swimming safety and water safety.

As swimmers become more comfortable in the water, they learn more strokes. The stroke called the *crawl* or *freestyle* is the fastest way to swim. This stroke, along with the *backstroke* and the *breaststroke*, are shown in the pictures.

Swimming competitions are held around the world. In the United States, many high schools, colleges, and private groups have swim teams. Swimmers work with a trainer to improve their speed. Swimming is also an Olympic sport. One of the most famous swimmers of recent years is Mark Spitz. Spitz won seven gold medals at the 1972 Olympic Games in Munich, West Germany. (*See* **Olympic Games.**)

Some swimmers train to swim long distances or for long periods of time. Swimmers have crossed the rough seas of the English Channel, for example. Most swimmers like to swim just for recreation and exercise. People of all ages swim to relax and to stay fit.

Caution: Everyone who swims should obey some simple safety rules. Don't swim right after you eat a meal. Don't dive into water you are not familiar with. Most important, never swim alone.

Four swimming strokes: the breaststroke (top left), the crawl (top right), the backstroke (bottom left), and the sidestroke (bottom right).

ELEVATION Feet

Over 10000
5000- 10000
2000- 5000
1000- 2000
0- 1000

MILES
0   40

WEST GERMANY

Basel

Winterthur

Zürich

St. Gallen

Lake Constance

AUSTRIA

LIECHTENSTEIN

JURA MOUNTAINS

Biel

Lake Biel

Neuchâtel

Lake Zürich

Lake of Neuchâtel

Bern ★

SWITZERLAND

Lucerne

FRANCE

Fribourg

Thun

Lake of Brienz

Lake Geneva

Lausanne

Lake of Thun

Interlaken

A L P S

St. Moritz

Geneva

N
W   E
S

Zermatt

ITALY

Lugano

Matterhorn
(14,690 ft.)

A street along the
Lake Zurich shore.

Switzerland

Capital: Bern
Area: 15,941 square miles (41,287 square kilometers)
Population (1985): about 6,457,000
Official languages: German, French, Italian

Switzerland is a small, mountainous country in western Europe. It is a world leader in banking and watchmaking. It is also famous for its beauty and its long tradition of peace.

Switzerland is completely surrounded by land. Its neighbors are West Germany, Austria, Liechtenstein, Italy, and France. The Jura Mountains run through its western part, and the Alps run through the east. The steep slopes and marvelous views attract skiers and climbers. Many of the highest peaks rise from deep, narrow valleys. Herders raise cattle and goats in these valleys. The animals' milk is used for making cheese and other dairy products.

Between the two mountain ranges, there is a lower area called the Swiss plateau. *Glaciers*—moving sheets of ice—have left lakes in the plateau. The largest are Lake Constance and Lake Geneva. Most of Switzerland's industry, agriculture, and large cities are in this region.

Over the years, many people from France, Germany, and Italy have settled in Switzerland. People of German descent make up the largest group. Their language is called Swiss German. The cities of Bern, Basel, and Zurich are in the German part of the nation. People of French descent make up the second-largest group. Most live in western Switzerland, next to France. The cities of Geneva and Lausanne are in this region. People of Italian descent live in the southeastern part of the nation.

Most Swiss land is not flat enough to be good farmland, so the Swiss have turned to banking and industry as ways to make a living. People from all over the world deposit money into Swiss banks. Swiss craftspeople are skilled in making jewelry, watches, and other delicate instruments. Switzerland also produces medicines and fine silk and cotton textiles. Swiss candymakers are known for their delicious chocolate.

Switzerland has been a neutral nation since 1515. A neutral nation does not take sides in a war and tries to stay out of wars. During World War II (1939 to 1945), many people seeking safety fled to Switzerland. Even though it is neutral, Switzerland keeps a well-trained army, and all young men must take military training.

Switzerland has not joined the United Nations, because the U.N. sometimes takes military action. But the Swiss city Geneva is the U.N.'s European headquarters.

symbiosis

Symbiosis means "living together." In nature, living things depend on one another for food, shelter, and many other needs. But symbiosis is about special ways of living very closely together. In a symbiotic relationship, the living things are together for a long time. Sometimes they help one another. Sometimes one is helped and the other is harmed. Sometimes one is helped and the other is neither helped nor hurt.

Mutualism is symbiosis where both kinds of living things are helped. Lichens are an example of mutualism. They are formed by a fungus and an alga living together so closely that they act like a single living thing. The alga carries out *photosynthesis*—making food from sunlight and water. Both the alga and the fungus use this food. The fungus covers the alga's cells and protects them from drying out. Together, the fungus and the alga can live in places where neither of them could live alone. (*See* **lichen**.)

Another example of mutualism is found between bacteria and plants. Certain bacteria live on the roots of bean plants and pea plants. The bacteria produce nitrogen compounds, which the plants need for growth. In return, the plants give the bacteria food and a good place to live. This relationship is so important that beans and peas do not grow well without the bacteria.

Oxpeckers are African birds that feed on ticks. Ticks are small creatures that feed on

The tiny wrasse swims inside the large fish's mouth, where it finds and eats parasites harmful to the large fish. In this kind of symbiosis, two animals seem to help each other.

the blood of live animals. So the oxpeckers adopt a large animal, such as an antelope, and ride on its back. When ticks land on the animal, the oxpeckers pull them out and eat them. In this relationship, the birds get food and a ride, and the animal gets rid of the ticks that harm it.

The termite is another creature that depends on mutualism to survive. Termites cannot digest the wood that they eat, but protists living in their stomachs can. By digesting the wood, the protists give both themselves and the termites food. The termites provide a safe place for the protists to live. Bacteria in the stomachs of cows help them digest their food. Humans have bacteria in their intestines that make certain vitamins. These relationships are forms of mutualism, too. (*See* **termite** and **protist**.)

Parasitism is symbiosis where one of the living things is harmed. The living thing that is helped is a *parasite,* and the living thing that is harmed is the *host*. The ticks that the oxpecker eats are parasites. They burrow their heads into the skin of an animal host and suck the animal's blood. As a tick feeds, its body swells. Ticks stay attached to a host until they are pulled off.

The mistletoe plant (yellow) takes nourishment from its host tree.

Some parasites kill their hosts. But those that do have to find a new host. As long as the parasite only weakens its host, it will have a place to live. (*See* **parasite.**)

Commensalism is a type of symbiosis in which one living thing is helped and the other is not affected. Sharks and remora fish are an example of commensalism. The remora has a suction cup on its head. The remora uses the suction cup to attach itself to the body of a shark. As the shark swims, the remora gets a free ride. It also gets bits of food from the shark's meals. The remora is helped, but the shark does not seem to be helped or hurt.

There are not many examples of commensalism. Some relationships that scientists used to call "commensalism" have turned out to be other kinds of symbiosis. As scientists watch living things closely, they learn more about how creatures help and harm one another. More observations of remoras and sharks may show that sharks actually are helped or harmed by remoras.

See also **ecology.**

symphony

A symphony is a particular kind of musical piece played by a large symphony orchestra. Most of the symphonies we hear today were written between 1750 and 1920. Only a few of today's composers write symphonies.

A symphony usually has four *movements*—parts. The first movement is often the longest and is played at a fast pace. The second movement is slower and often sounds sad. The third movement often has the rhythm of a lively dance. The last movement is usually the fastest and most lighthearted.

Joseph Haydn, a great composer of the 1700s, wrote more than 100 symphonies. Wolfgang Amadeus Mozart, who also lived in the 1700s, wrote more than 40. Their symphonies are short, each taking 15 to 30 minutes to play.

In the 1800s, Ludwig van Beethoven wrote longer symphonies. Many people believe that his nine symphonies are the greatest ever written. Other important symphonies were written by Franz Schubert, Johannes Brahms, and Gustav Mahler.

See also **Haydn, Franz Joseph; Mozart, Wolfgang Amadeus; Beethoven, Ludwig van;** and **orchestra**.)

synthetic fabric

Natural fabrics—such as linen, cotton, wool, and silk—come from plant fibers, animal hair, and moth cocoons. A synthetic fabric is made from substances put together by chemists in a laboratory. These fabrics include acrylic, polyester, and nylon. Rayon is often classed as a synthetic or man-made fabric, too. It is made by treating the cellulose in wood and cotton with chemicals. Synthetic fibers are woven and knitted into all kinds of fabrics. They give strength to cords, fire hoses, and automobile tires.

Synthetic fabrics were first developed as substitutes for expensive and scarce natural fabrics. Today, synthetics are the preferred materials in some cases. Cloth is often a blend of natural and synthetic fibers so that it has the best features of each.

Synthetics can be strong, soft, shiny, stretchy, and lightweight. Some synthetic fibers absorb bright colors well and fade very little, even when exposed to sunlight regularly. This makes them a good choice for curtains. Many synthetics are shaped by very high heat. Clothing made from these synthetics does not wrinkle or sag out of shape. Except for rayon, synthetic fabrics do not absorb water. This helps them dry quickly and resist stains—good features for carpets and tablecloths. Since synthetics are not made from natural products, they do not rot and do not attract insects.

Synthetics also have some poor qualities. In a fire, they burn or melt more quickly than natural fabrics and give off poisonous gases. In hot weather, clothing made of synthetics is uncomfortable because your sweat cannot evaporate easily through the cloth. In

Long strands of a synthetic material are woven or knit into synthetic fabric.

cold weather, some synthetics do not do a good job of keeping you warm.

Each kind of synthetic is made from its own blend of materials. First, the materials are melted or mixed with a liquid. The mixture can be shaped into any form. To make fibers, the mixture is forced through small holes called *spinnerets.* As the mixture passes through the spinnerets, it hardens into long threads. These threads are twisted together to make a thicker thread. The threads are then woven or knit into fabric.

Sometimes, the mixture is not forced through tiny holes but through a long, narrow slit. This produces a thin, strong, flexible sheet that can be sewed like fabric.

Kinds of Synthetics Many synthetic fibers are known by the names given them by their manufacturers. Often, only the manufacturer knows the fiber's formula, and no one can use the formula without permission. Chemists are always trying to come up with new formulas for synthetics.

Rayon was invented in 1884 by a French scientist, Hilaire Chardonnet. He developed rayon as a substitute for silk, an expensive natural fabric. For many years, rayon was known as "artificial silk." The first rayon fabrics were shiny and did not look good after washing. They were used for women's stockings, underclothes, and dresses. Today, rayon shrinks if washed in hot water, but it takes dyes well, drapes nicely, and comes in a wide range of finishes. It is used for clothing, curtains, and furniture coverings.

Nylon is a strong fiber that lasts a long time. It was invented in 1938 by an American scientist named Wallace Carothers. Since then, many nylon formulas have been developed. Nylon is made from materials that come from coal, water, air, petroleum, and natural gas. Nylon products include women's stockings, underclothes, swimsuits, and dresses. Nylon is also used for rugs, parachutes, tires, ropes, and fishing lines.

Acrylic is made from petroleum and used to make numerous products, including fabrics. Many acrylic fabrics are known by the manufacturers' names for them—such as Orlon, Acrilan, and Dynel. Acrylic fabrics dry quickly without shrinking, fading, or wrinkling. Sweaters, rugs, and blankets are often made of acrylic.

Polyester, too, is made from petroleum and is made into many useful products, including fabrics. Polyester is often used in "wash-and-wear" clothing, because it dries easily, and keeps its shape. Polyester fabrics are also used for furniture, curtains, and rugs. Polyester is often blended with cotton to make sheets, pillowcases, and shirts. It is mixed with wool to make suit cloth. *Dacron* and *Kodel* are the names of polyester fabrics made by two different companies.

Fiberglass is made of very thin threads of glass that are woven or matted together. Fiberglass is fireproof and often used for curtains. People do not use much fiberglass for clothing, because splinters from it can irritate the skin.

Other synthetic fibers include *olefin* and *spandex.* Olefin is used for carpets and cords. Spandex is a stretchy fiber often used in formfitting clothing.

Synthetics are used in all the products pictured here—tires, rope, tents, sleeping bags, rugs, and many kinds of clothing.

Syria

Capital: Damascus
Area: 71,467 square miles (185,100 square kilometers)
Population (1985): about 10,535,000
Official language: Arabic

Syria is a country in the Middle East. Its history goes back thousands of years. Syria has been the home of some of the world's great civilizations.

On the west, Syria borders Lebanon and the Mediterranean Sea. Turkey lies on Syria's north, and Iraq is on the east. Israel and Jordan are to the south.

Syria's coastal region has plenty of rain for farming. Farther east, mountain ranges block the moist winds from the sea. Syria has several river valleys and fertile plains. The Euphrates River Valley runs across the east and north. The Orontes River brings water to the plains east of the mountains. The plains and valleys are irrigated and planted with wheat, barley, cotton, sugar beets, fruits, and vegetables.

Syria's economy depends on agriculture and oil. Glass, cotton cloth, and chemical products are manufactured there, too.

Most Syrian people live along the coast or in the western valleys and plains. About half the people live in villages and work on farms. The rest live in Damascus, the capital, Aleppo, and other cities.

Syria's location has played an important role in its history. Ancient trade routes between Europe, North Africa, the Middle East, and Asia crossed Syria. Traders helped spread Syrian crafts and learning to other parts of the Mediterranean world.

People have lived in Syria since 4500 B.C. The Semites settled there about 3500 B.C. Many others have passed through or invaded Syria, including the Assyrians, Babylonians, Persians, Greeks, and Romans. During the 500s, Syria became part of the Byzantine Empire. In 636, Arabs invaded Syria and brought the new religion of Islam. Today, about three out of four Syrians are Muslims—followers of Islam.

In 1516, the Ottoman Turks added Syria to their empire. The Turks ruled Syria for 400 years. In 1920, France was given control of Syria. Syria became independent from France in 1946.

Since then, Syria has had several changes of government. It has also been involved in the conflict in the Middle East between Israel and the Arab countries.

A mosque in Damascus, Syria's capital and largest city.

Feet above sea level

5,000
2,000
1,000
500
0
Below sea level

0   100 Miles
0   100 Kilometers

TURKEY

Aleppo
Latakia
Khabur River
Euphrates River
Hama
Deir ez Zor
Homs
Mediterranean Sea
SYRIA
LEBANON
ISRAEL
Damascus
IRAQ
Es Suweida
JORDAN

N
W   E
S